DON'T WALK ALONE

DON'T WALK ALONE

Understanding
the Divine Gift of Connection
while Navigating Shame

ERIKA NORDFELT, MA, LCPC

PLAIN SIGHT PUBLISHING
An imprint of Cedar Fort, Inc.
Springville, Utah

© 2022 Erika Nordfelt
All rights reserved.

No part of this book may be reproduced in any form whatsoever, whether by graphic, visual, electronic, film, microfilm, tape recording, or any other means, without prior written permission of the publisher, except in the case of brief passages embodied in critical reviews and articles.

This is not an official publication of The Church of Jesus Christ of Latter-day Saints. The opinions and views expressed herein belong solely to the author and do not necessarily represent the opinions or views of Cedar Fort, Inc. Permission for the use of sources, graphics, and photos is also solely the responsibility of the author.

ISBN 13: 978-1-4621-4148-7

Published by Plain Sight Publishing, an imprint of Cedar Fort, Inc.
2373 W. 700 S., STE 1, Springville, UT 84663
Distributed by Cedar Fort, Inc., www.cedarfort.com

Library of Congress Control Number: 2022941575

Cover design by Courtney Proby
Cover design © 2022 Cedar Fort, Inc.
Edited by Laurie Campbell

Printed in the United States of America

10 9 8 7 6 5 4 3 2 1

Printed on acid-free paper

Dedication

Sometimes we lack motivation and we somehow have to muscle through and figure it out on our own. Sometimes we are gifted people in our lives who give us the motivation we need. Heidi, you were my gift. Best sister/editor one could hope for.

Contents

INTRODUCTION 1
CHAPTER 1: Connection 5
CHAPTER 2: Connection and Shame 15
CHAPTER 3: Shame 33
CHAPTER 4: Deflecting Shame 45
CHAPTER 5: Perfectionism 55
CHAPTER 6: Self-Awareness 71
CHAPTER 7: Vulnerability, Empathy, and Boundaries 79
CHAPTER 8: Common Humanity 95
CHAPTER 9: Perspective and Unconditional Love 103
CHAPTER 10: Mindfulness 115
CHAPTER 11: Hope 133
CONCLUSION 151
BIBLIOGRAPHY 153
ABOUT THE AUTHOR . . . .

Introduction

Because this book is founded on principles of vulnerability and authenticity, I front-load with my story of writing it. The idea came to me in 2018. The writing, editing, finding a publisher, rewriting, and more editing took years. Those years coincided with a lot of personal and spiritual change for me. I started writing as a very devout and traditional Christian. I was raised and taught the principles of that religion, attended church every Sunday, prayed, read scriptures, and served in different volunteer capacities within the church. I became a Mental Health Therapist at a Christian university. This work had a huge influence on my writing. At that point, my book was very focused on linking powerful psychological concepts to Christian teachings and doctrine. The process of writing was deeply meaningful for me because psychology was a large part of my world and religious concepts were even more so. Finding the parallel between the two was special and I felt inspired to help others with my ideas. Over those years, my experience with spirituality, God, and connection continued to evolve. I had struggled through lots of unfortunate experiences and my feelings about God changed greatly to the point that I could no longer remain a member of any specific church. This was a move toward more integrity for me. The full story is probably best told in another setting or a different book. Suffice it to say, I could no longer be true to myself and my religion. Yet, during this time, the writing and publishing of my book continued to move forward. So here I am, trying to find my way through my spiritual crisis with grace and at the same time, preparing to publish a really Christian book. I mean, super Christian. I quoted Bible leaders and scriptures and told stories about different Christian historical figures. It was sopping wet with religiosity! This became super distressing for me. Yet if I was making a big spiritual change based on my integrity, I could not also be the face of a book that no longer represented me. That would *not* show integrity.

However, changing the book or dropping it presented its own struggle. All that I had put into that book was powerful and for those who still believed as I did, it would have been helpful. The tie between mental health concepts and Christian doctrine is what made it good. So I sat with that dilemma for a while. Sometimes crying, sometimes eating too much food, sometimes just sitting. I could just publish it anyway with a disclaimer of "Here is my very Christian book. I hope it helps you in your very Christian lifestyle. Also, I am not a practicing Christian anymore." Ha? That is not a great marketing strategy. Not only would that not be wise for my publisher, it would discredit a lot of the book because I was no longer a believer. Maybe I could get a coauthor or just give it to someone else. I could be the ghostwriter. I didn't have to be the face of the book. But that wouldn't work either. The book was chock-full of my personal and professional stories. Just as much as the book was Christian, it was also very me.

So I, with a very supportive publishing team, made the hard call to rewrite and make the book more general nonfiction. That is what the book has now become. I speak from a nuanced Christian perspective. I still talk about Jesus and even quote various scriptures. In addition, I talk about Buddha and Maya Angelou and even quote Kung Fu Panda. I have redesigned this book to be universally relatable to all humans that seek out spirituality, connection, and well-being. I haven't forgotten my religious roots. I hope Christians can still benefit from my ideas. Now I can be true to myself as I continue my effort to create connective and healing moments in people's lives.

Connection comes in many special forms; connection with others, connection with nature, connection with self, and connection with God or any higher power. I also feel a connection to energy or life itself at times.

INTRODUCTION

Connection brings more meaning to life. That meaning can create a domino effect that enhances our perspective on living. Most importantly, it builds an understanding of self and a greater belief in our intrinsic value.

The ideas presented in this book are intended to add to, but not replace, the many useful and effective therapeutic treatment methods that already exist. This book is a good resource for mending emotional wounds, but it is not a complete guide for those with significant mental health concerns. If you, or someone you know, is seriously struggling with a mental health disorder, it is best to seek out professional help.

The book is designed to provide opportunities to reflect on "self" and personalize the message to your circumstances. Each chapter is followed by a "practice" section with questions and exercises that will allow you, the reader, to further implement or understand the material in the context of your own life. For some, it may be helpful to read the book with a notebook nearby. If you take the time to answer the questions and reflect on them, the concepts will be far more effective.

I hope to help. As a champion of the notion of "worth," I have a deep love for all humans. Every person on earth is valuable. I know that I am valuable. And even though you and I do not know each other personally, I know that you are valuable. As a therapist, if there were one thing I could help people internalize and believe it would be that we each deserve joy and a sense of belonging. We need connection to enhance that joy.

CHAPTER 1

Connection

It was the winter of 2009. I was nearing the end of my graduate program in counseling. I had 300 hours left of my internship (which was a part-time job with no pay) and was taking three additional classes. My husband was also in graduate school and working, trying to support our small family of three. We had to toggle our schedules to make work and school and internships function without getting any childcare for our two-and-a-half-year-old. We were both very involved with volunteer positions with our church that required hours and hours of work each week. I was pregnant and tired, stressed by school, overwhelmed by church stuff, and dealing with a constant feeling of inadequacy to measure up to it all. A good way for me to de-stress was by taking a bath, and that semester we went through a lot of bath water. There was one particular day I felt beside myself with emotion and I couldn't handle it on my own anymore. I needed help. I needed to talk.

I decided to call my sister who had survived her own stressful life load. At one point she also had been in grad school, while raising two small kids, working full time, and volunteering at church. I knew she would understand and I was desperate for magic words of wisdom to help me. So I called and we talked for a long time. The most powerful part of the conversation that stuck with me was this simple exchange: "Rach, how did you do it? How did you manage everything and not crumble?" She said simply, "I don't know. I have no magic secret for you. I just know that it was really hard and I understand what you're going through." I had called my sister with hopes of wisdom and advice and she gave me none, but somehow I still felt better. There was no specific solution to my problem. What healed my heart that day was that I could be completely open with her, share all of my emotions and struggles, and that she *got it*. She understood and loved me anyway. I felt better about myself and I felt less alone with my struggle. Turns out I didn't need the magic words of wisdom. I needed empathy.

When you hear the word "connection," what comes to mind? Synergy, energy, closeness, warmth, or something along those lines? For many people, connection is an inviting idea. However, for many others, the word "connection" conjures up feelings of fear, discomfort, vulnerability, or anxiety. Most of us fall into one of these groups, or possibly a combination of both.

Connection can be experienced in many ways. We can feel connected to another person. We can feel connected to a higher power or energy source. We can feel connected to nature or other life forms. We can also feel deeply connected to ourselves, which is probably the hardest to achieve. All of these forms of connection bring us a feeling of being alive and present. It is invigorating. For this book, I will mainly focus on connections with other people. However, all forms of connection are valuable and enhance our lives. Connection is a gateway to meaning-making.

Sincere interpersonal human connection requires three elements:

1. One person shares themselves in a vulnerable and personal way.

2. Their ideas and feelings are welcomed by the other person or persons and possibly reciprocated, or there is some type of shared energy.

3. Afterward, all people involved have a new feeling of closeness and emotional intimacy.

CHAPTER 1: CONNECTION

In those moments of connection, both parties are lifted and changed, even if only in a small way. These are the experiences that fuel joy and contentment.

In every moment of sincere connection, we grow closer to each other, which invites powerful spiritual energy. I feel like that is God or at least a divine energy that is designed to bring humans together. It is a spiritual or Godlike experience because it requires sharing our true, honest hearts. Some settings create an ideal environment for that to happen like some church or school groups, but in general, this way of interacting is intentionally and unintentionally avoided. For many of us, sincere connection is difficult because it requires us to be open and vulnerable. Those two words can sound as inviting as a bear attack. It can be really scary! If I open up then they will know how I feel and I work very hard all day long to keep that locked up in my "deepest, darkest secrets" vault. However, if we remain disconnected we will always struggle emotionally. Brené Brown says that "we are hardwired to connect with others, it's what gives purpose and meaning in our lives, and without it, there is suffering" (Brown, *Daring Greatly*).

Connection is innate. We are not meant to live this life alone. It is our relationships and our capacity for connection that set us apart from the rest of God's creations. Some people may say, "I really connect with my dog. I connect with him more than any human." And I am all about a special relationship with animals.

My husband was not a pet person. We had several dogs that were slightly neurotic and needy. He never cared for them—never really cared for any pets up to that point. Then one day we got a small orange calico kitten and I saw him bond with her in a similar fashion to our four children. He discovered this new love for the tiny helpless ball of fur. It was surprising and adorable. Yet as much as he loves our cat, he cannot bond with her on the intimate level he can with another person because that connection does not require vulnerability. It is that vulnerability and open honesty that forges the bond of interpersonal connection.

So why does vulnerability have to be the key ingredient? Why can't we talk and share within our comfort zones and grow that way? For the obvious reason that growth doesn't happen in any comfort zone. In Kung Fu Panda 3, Master Shi Fu tells Po, "If you only do what you can do, you will never be more than you are now" (Stevenson, *Kung Fu Panda*). You gotta love great power and insight communicated through a wise and aged cartoon tortoise. When we share our stories, our honest stories, we experience emotion, whether it be fear or excitement, or sorrow. The very nature of emotion is vulnerable.

Now let me be clear about what I mean by honest stories. The stories we tell from our hearts are not travel logs or family updates or logistics of the day. They are not political likes or dislikes. They are not complaining about work. Honest open stories always involve personal experience and the *emotion* it evokes. That is what makes it personal and often so hidden or protected. However, when we remain protective of that story, we feel disconnected and alone. It is through the act of sharing that we can process the story, create meaning, heal, and recognize we are all together in this wild and crazy life.

Vulnerability requires courage. There is a risk people will judge us or make fun of or even betray our trust and tell other people. So yes, we must be brave, but that is where the payoff comes in. If I build up enough courage to share my story with the right people (and I stress the right people, because not everyone is deserving of our stories) and I find myself more connected and confident in myself, I am more likely to repeat the process because fear did not triumph.

In college, I had an experience while working at a ropes course during the summer at Grand Targhee Resort in Idaho. One particular day, I was working at the top of the zip line. It was my job to clip in and secure each person to the rope before they zipped off down the line. There was a young girl, Kate, probably in her early teens, who was next in line. Kate was terrified and hesitant even before she got to me, which was on top of a 30-foot pole platform. It took a lot of coaxing and reassurance just to get her up on the platform. By that time her anxiety was in full tilt, just short of a panic attack. Once she reached me, I quickly clipped her in and had her sit to calm down. She was convinced that the rope and cable were not going to hold her, that she would fall and die. I told her to take deep breaths, to look me straight in the eye, and listen. I began to explain all the features of the equipment and reassure her of its safety. "This rope is hooked into the harness, which I have double-checked. It's tight and secure. It will not

CHAPTER 1: CONNECTION

fall off of you. These carabiners are locked. A carabiner can hold about 225 pounds and two carabiners are holding you to the rope."

With some time and a bit more coaxing, she began to calm down. I could tell she was beginning to believe what I was saying. Trust was forming. She was not going to die. Now she just had to muster up the courage to scooch off the platform, which took even more encouragement and convincing. In the end, she had to trust that it would be worth the risk. She had to believe that it was going to be as fun as I said. So she took a deep breath and pushed off. Then, for the next 300 feet of the zip line, she screamed at the top of her lungs. This was a joyful scream full of excitement and energy. As soon as she finished and was taken off the line, she ran back to the bottom of my pole, ready to do it all over again. Once she climbed back to me, she said, with great enthusiasm, "That was the most fun I have ever had! You were right." For this young teenager, it was a huge risk and she had to find the courage she didn't even know was there. In the end, that surge of adrenaline and rush of excitement were completely worth it.

Courage is an interesting thing. The root of the word courage is *cor* which is Latin for heart. Brené Brown stated, "Courage originally meant to speak one's mind by telling all one's heart" (Brown, *Gifts of Imperfection*). I love that! The risk involved for us to connect requires our full honest hearts to get through, but the payoff is worth it. Just as Kate received a chemical "high" of adrenaline when she went on the zip line, we receive similar chemical rewards for connection. Our brains contribute all sorts of chemicals that affect our emotions. When we hear sincere stories that evoke emotion, our brains release oxytocin, which is nicknamed the bonding chemical. It creates a feeling of closeness to other people. I joke that connection can get you "high on oxy."

I have had several experiences with female youth groups back when I was involved in my old church where we would enjoy a week-long camping experience. Part of that camp was a "testimony meeting" where the girls would share their spiritual stories, including their thoughts about God and meaningful experiences from the week. This meeting can often be emotional and very meaningful for those in attendance. After the meeting, there was always an increase in energy. The rest of the night was usually a bit crazy because they were all hyped up on the bonding chemicals. It feels good to feel close to each other.

Wait, there are even more chemicals! Our brains are also hardwired for stories. Stories with a beginning, middle, and end. Hence, the reason we love movies, books, and other story-like entertainment. When we hear a complete story with a resolution at the end, our brains also release serotonin and dopamine, more feel-good chemicals. Hearing another person's complete and honest story gives us more understanding and insight which help make us feel bonded and happy. Whether it be God or evolution or something else, we are designed to need and crave connection and then have a complete physical reaction when it happens.

I have been working as a Mental Health Therapist for nearly a decade. Vulnerability and connection are topics that come up in nearly every one of my therapy sessions with clients. The leading reason most of the people I work with resist being open is the fear that they will be judged. They give reasons like, "They won't look at me the same," "They will think I'm weak or crazy," "I don't want to burden them with my problems," or, "if I tell them these things, they will know too much," (as if the listener now has highly sensitive information and will misuse it). So the resistance wins and people remain closed off and distanced.

Then I ask, "What is it like to be on the receiving end of vulnerability?" and, "In those experiences, do you judge that person or feel like they are weak?"

(As a small caveat, I will be referring to clients I work with or have worked with throughout this book. As a way of maintaining confidentiality and protecting their stories and identity, I have changed all the names and, in some cases, changed identifying details.)

I did this in a particular session with a young man named Jack. Jack was in college with a large class load. He was married, about to be a father, and had the weight of the world on his shoulders. His presenting issue when he first came in was extreme anxiety. Jack believed he had to live perfectly to gain love and approval. Perfectionism is almost always coupled with anxiety. Nothing Jack did was ever focused on an inward pleasure. He only operated out of the need to please others. I suggested that in between our sessions, he go home and watch some

CHAPTER 1: CONNECTION

videos that built on the idea of vulnerability and shame. Jack came back the next week and immediately started talking about the videos.

"I watched the videos," he said

"You did? Great! What did you like? What did you not like?"

"Well," he said with a long sigh, "I watched and there was this one part where the lady talks about how vulnerability makes people beautiful. I do not understand that at all! When I talk about my weaknesses, how does that make me beautiful?"

I immediately knew what he was referring to. One of the videos I suggested was Brené Brown's first TED Talk which was a viral sensation. In that video, she talks about people she called "wholehearted." These are people that her research showed to be living more fulfilling and authentic lives. She pointed out that a huge difference between the "wholehearted" and other people was that "they fully embraced vulnerability. They believed that what made them vulnerable made them beautiful" (Brown, "The Power of Vulnerability").

So Jack, who had a firm belief that vulnerability is weakness and that being authentic to his emotions would only highlight his imperfections, had a knee-jerk reaction against this idea of beauty.

I asked, "Jack, I want you to tell me a time where you have been on the receiving end of openness, a time when someone shared personal and vulnerable things with you."

"Okay," he said, "My wife has done that with me. There was a specific time she talked to me about something she had never told anyone else in her life."

"How did it feel being the one person she had ever shared that with?"

He said, "It felt special. I felt honored that she trusted me enough to share something so personal."

Then I asked, "How did you feel about *her* when she shared it? Did you think she was weak?"

"I felt more love for her because she was sharing so much of herself with me. I knew that was hard."

"In that moment, did you see her as beautiful?"

"Yes. It was beautiful because it was all of her. I love everything about her."

Then I asked, "How do you think that experience of her opening up changed your relationship?"

He said, "I felt closer to her. It had bonded us more."

In that experience, Jack saw beauty in the honesty of his wife. It brought them closer together and her courage was celebrated by him. That discussion began a shift for Jack. He could then consider viewing himself and his vulnerabilities like he viewed his wife's. He could understand that these perceived "weaknesses" were just a part of his real, authentic self. It's safe to assume that if I could have a conversation with Jack's wife about this same experience, she would agree that even though it was hard to open up, her marriage was strengthened because of it.

As we struggle to understand the connection and how to practice it more in our lives, it is crucial to remember that we can draw on our divine capacity to practice it more.

In Matthew 5:14–15, Jesus taught, "Ye are the light of the world. A city that is set on a hill cannot be hid. Neither do men light a candle, and put it under a bushel, but on a candlestick; and it giveth light unto all that are in the house." We have been placed on a hill. Our light can light all those in the house. This is our full light and our full selves. It does not say that we put our candle on a candlestick, but we make sure that the drippy wax part is facing the wall so no one can see it.

As my spiritual journey has evolved throughout my life, I have come to know only one thing; I don't know anything. I used to profess to know God and know his plan and know details of life on earth and life after death. So much of my life was built on those things. As I matured and learned more of the complexities of being human, I could no longer hold certainty of anything. Life is freaking messy! Some days life feels synergetic and everything's coming together, and it seems to make beautiful sense. Other days, it's an exploding pressure cooker with projectile food pieces flinging in every direction. However, I do feel and believe that something connects all living things. There is an energy that links us all and I choose to believe it is God.

Practice

- Think of a time when you felt a connection the strongest? What happened? What or whom did you feel a connection to? Afterward, how did you feel? How did you feel about what or whom you were connecting with

- What did your body feel like? *(I will often ask about physical sensations with emotions. This is because our body acts as the first responder to emotion and when we are more self-aware, those sensations are signals that allow us to understand what we are feeling. We call them feelings for a reason: because we feel them in our bodies.*

- What are your thoughts on connection in general? Where does it show up in your life? Where is it lacking? Are there places where connection happens naturally?

- Does connection have any spiritual ties for you? What and why?

CHAPTER 2

Connection and Shame

IF CONNECTION IS THIS IMPORTANT EXPERIENCE THAT BONDS US together, what keeps us from doing it more? Well, vulnerability is part of it. But what makes people feel vulnerable? Why is one person vulnerable one way and another person vulnerable in the complete opposite way? The answer is shame. We cannot talk about connection and understand it unless we understand its most diabolical contender: shame. I believe shame to be one of the most powerful emotions. Shame is best friends with fear, anxiety, and depression. This gang is in direct opposition to connection. These extremes either lift us toward each other and toward God, or they press us down. Shame flattens us down and goes to work on keeping us there. It is corrosive and destructive. Yet experiencing shame is very normal for most humans (excluding certain personality and developmental disorders). It is normal, yet the message it sends is not true.

One common misunderstanding is the difference between shame and guilt. These two are often used interchangeably in our language, especially in religious texts. They are very different and have separate purposes. Guilt is associated with regret for an action or experience. Guilt is, "I did something bad or wrong." Guilt can be a good thing. It can move us toward change and progress. In a lot of Christian doctrines, guilt is integral to the atonement. It helps move people toward repentance or making amends with God. A common joke for Catholics is this: "My body is a temple . . . more like a Catholic church. Full of bread, wine, and guilt." In 2 Corinthians, this is called godly sorrow. Guilt is a tool that is meant to shape and mold us as we progress and learn. This idea is far more universal, even outside any spiritual context. When I get into a disagreement with someone I love and I say something hurtful, whether I mean to or not, guilt will motivate me to apologize. In sessions, I tell people to pay attention to guilt. Guilt is signaling to your body to do something important. When we develop better intuition, we can use that signal to improve our relationships, emotions, and experiences. Organic guilt is useful.

Shame, on the other hand, is destructive and dangerous. Shame tells us that because we did something bad, we *are* something bad. It always targets our sense of self and worth. We can easily move from guilt to shame. Guilt is meant to move us forward, but when regret turns to despair, we start to move backward. Shame keeps us away from growth and progress because we do not feel we are capable of change, or even worthy of it. Shame creates a script that is stuck on repeat saying, "You are not _____ enough." This clever phrase allows us to insert anything important into the blank to fit our situation. "I'm not: smart enough, capable enough, likable enough, attractive enough." Or, the most simple yet most common, "I'm not good enough." Shame feeds off our insecurities to maintain its power and dominance. It is what makes comparison a mighty battle and self-criticism a household name.

I worked with a client named Stacy who grew up with a mother with undiagnosed bipolar disorder and severe codependency issues. She told me of how, at a certain age, her mother started to treat her differently. Her mother would start to say things like, "How could you do that to me? Don't you love me at all?" and Stacy had only disobeyed her mother by wearing her hair in a ponytail to school. Stacy liked ponytails. Over the years, Stacy's mom continued and increased her criticism of Stacy. Comments become more hurtful and damaging like "You will never be good enough" or "What you are doing is stupid." Stacy was not a rebellious teen. She worked hard in school and got good grades. After high school, she started college and tried to do it with a smile. However, early down the line she adopted all the criticism from her mother and made it her own. The small germ of shame turned into extreme anxiety and depression.

Though Stacy was competent in many ways, she battled against that shame. She saw me for several years and during that time, she met a wonderful young man and got married. The shame never tested her as it did once she was married because she took all that self-criticism and doubt and projected it onto her husband. Projection is when person A believes that person B feels the same way about person A as person A feels about themselves. Stacy kept expecting her husband to act and react the same way as her mother, which was rooted in her shame about herself. Stacy's shame was disguised as her mother's. But there was hope for Stacy. She had dedicated herself to understanding her shame, and as she worked, her anxiety and depression lifted, and her marriage got stronger.

GODLY SORROW

When I was deep in my research for this book, I found a scriptural reference that perfectly illustrates this point. The ironic thing is that it was from the apostle Paul in 2 Corinthians. I am not a big fan of Paul. Though I love reading the gospels and reading about Christ, I lose my enthusiasm for Paul's teachings. However, 2 Corinthians 7:10 is insightful. Paul says, "For godly sorrow (guilt) worketh repentance to salvation not to be repented of: but the sorrow of the world (shame) worketh death."

Godly sorrow is feeling sorrowful for wrong actions. It is necessary for us to feel this way. As humans, when we feel something negative, we naturally try to move away from it. This is a method of self-preservation. However, there are many directions in which we can move. Guilt should move us forward. Shame moves us backward or keeps us stuck in place. Shame does this by convincing us we failed. This is often where shame teams up with fear and other discouraging emotions. I will get more into fear in Chapter 4. Guilt should indeed make us feel bad but not make us feel like a failure. When I went to college, I had to learn what worked and what didn't work for my study habits. I quickly realized that I could not do my homework at home. There were far too many social distractions there and I could not focus. I had to hide in a corner cubby on the third floor of the library. I was far more successful in my work that way. So on days when I chose to spend more time at home being social and less time in the library, which resulted in lower scores on tests or projects, I had to own the results. I felt bad about the outcome and learned from it.

I learned to avoid going home in between certain classes and to schedule my social time better so I could still "fill my social bucket." It took several years, but by the time I graduated, I had fine-tuned my ability to study. I did that through a series of good and bad choices. I also had to learn how to contend with the feeling of shame that told me I was a bad student when I got bad grades. I had to assure myself that I was not a bad student, I just didn't prepare as well as I knew how. Or, at times when I *did* prepare well but still got bad grades, I had to learn that it was okay. I wasn't stupid. I just wasn't going to be highly successful in all things, like statistics, for example. I was still good enough as a person. My value was untouched. My mistakes and struggles as a student did not need to sink to a deeper level of shame.

For me, being a student was not a "soft spot" for shame. I probably had more resilience to shame. We all have different areas where we are more prone to feel shame or guilt. It is good to understand both areas for ourselves. Sometimes we can learn from our guilt-prone areas to help with the more shame-prone ones.

When it comes to bigger struggles, like mental health problems or relationship struggles, it is really hard to keep guilt from turning into shame. When there is more "weight" to the struggle, it easily finds its way to shame. With addiction, it takes a lot of diligent shame resilience practice to maintain adequate guilt that leads us to Christ in a way where we can change, be healed, and maintain our worth along the way. I feel like the atonement is intended to make us feel valuable and important. Guilt can lead us to those emotions, while shame ruins that experience and steals our hope. Guilt should foster hope.

- "I messed up, but I'm going to keep trying."

- "I felt depressed all day today, but maybe tomorrow will be different."

- "I had a panic attack again about work stresses, but I am working on my stress coping and I can get through this."

CHAPTER 2: CONNECTION AND SHAME

- "I lost my patience with my kids again because I am so stressed, but I can apologize and do better next time."

Each of these examples acknowledges the struggle. There is no justification or minimizing the struggle. Most importantly, there is hope that it can get better.

Sometimes these ideas can be misconstrued. When I talk about self-acceptance and practicing self-compassion, people resist. Some think that by accepting themselves and their "weaknesses" they are just giving up or they see it as an excuse to stop trying. I put so much emphasis on the need to challenge the shame and be more kind that we miss the very real and essential need for guilt. Let me make one thing clear: **choosing guilt over shame is not the easy way out.** It doesn't mean becoming so accepting and laid back that nothing matters. Guilt is not being so forgiving for all shortcomings that there is no need for learning and growing. Guilt is tough. But guilt does not damage us as shame does. It refines and strengthens us. With guilt, there is hope and love and a pathway to becoming our true selves.

Core Values

I see guilt as an inner barometer where our body is signaling our mind that we are out of alignment with our core values. Inner compass, intuition, the knowing, integrity, I call them core values. These are a set of values that develop individually for each person. When we are out of touch with those values, our bodies feel it. That is the discomfort that shows up with guilt. It is important and gets our attention to make things right. When we can realign ourselves, we maintain hope.

It is worth taking the time to define your core values. Not only is this a great introspective process, but it can also act as a tool to help navigate experiences and relationships as well as help inform decisions and boundaries. When I introduce this concept in sessions, I emphasize that core values are values that are integral to the self. They are not the values you have been told to have from outside sources. So, at least to start, you need to set aside the messages you have been given throughout your life about what you should value. That is not to say those things aren't valuable, they just may not be part of your core.

Core values already exist in the self and are part of what motivates our actions, interactions, and more. These are the things we have a hard time letting go of, or the things we want to teach our children. These are often things that cause contention or at least confrontation because we are willing to fight for these ideas. Yet you have to take time to assess these ideas to make sure that the values are not sourced from fear or anxiety.

You start by looking at a list of value words. This list was from a Brené Brown "Dare to Lead" training.

Accountability
Achievement
Adaptability
Adventure
Altruism
Ambition
Authenticity
Balance
Beauty
Being the best
Belonging
Career
Caring
Collaboration
Commitment
Community
Compassion
Competence
Confidence
Connection
Contentment
Contribution
Cooperation
Courage
Creativity
Curiosity
Dignity
Diversity
Environment
Efficiency
Equality
Ethics
Excellence
Fairness
Faith
Family
Financial stability
Forgiveness
Freedom
Friendship
Fun
Future generations
Generosity
Giving back
Grace
Gratitude

CHAPTER 2: CONNECTION AND SHAME

Growth
Harmony
Health
Home
Honesty
Hope
Humility
Humor
Inclusion
Independence
Initiative
Integrity
Intuition
Job security
Joy
Justice
Kindness
Knowledge
Leadership
Learning
Legacy
Leisure
Love
Loyalty
Making a difference
Nature
Openness
Optimism
Order
Parenting
Patience
Patriotism
Peace
Perseverance
Personal fulfillment
Power

Pride
Recognition
Reliability
Resourcefulness
Respect
Responsibility
Risk-taking
Safety
Security
Self-discipline
Self-expression Self-respect
Serenity
Service
Simplicity
Spirituality
Sportsmanship Stewardship
Success
Teamwork
Thrift
Time
Tradition
Travel
Trust
Truth
Understanding Uniqueness
Usefulness
Vision
Vulnerability
Wealth
Well-being
Wholeheartedness Wisdom
Write your own:
_____
_____
_____
_____

Go through the list and mark the ones that stand out. Then narrow down your list to those you find most important. Ideally, you want to end with a list of six values, with the three most important at the top of the list. You may see that some words are similar. Some people group the words and decide on one word to represent the whole. Words have power as well as different meanings or symbolism for each person. Be sure to choose words that resonate. Then reassess your list and make sure they source from a sense of self, not fear or anxiety. Take your time with this process. Observe yourself over time. It is helpful to ask, "What values are showing up for me right now?" The idea is that when you are living in line with your core values, you are your most true self. Also known as living within your integrity.

My top values are respect, authenticity, and love/connection. Not very surprising, I'm sure. I didn't realize that respect was such an important value until I saw it showing up in my behavior. I noticed it everywhere when I started looking. I had always acted this way, but I could finally understand the value behind my actions. Things like making sure my kids and I always say "thank you" or are always aware of others' boundaries and comfort levels. Make sure to always return messages or calls, and do it quickly because that is more respectful. Of course, all of this hinges on my definition of what respect is, and that definition is so motivating for me.

Identifying core values also gives us more insight into our relationships. We would like it if our partners had all the same core values. That would make things so much easier. But even if you value similar things, your core values most likely won't be the same. One summer my family was at an amusement park. There was a group of teens bouncing around the park cutting in line. My sister-in-law saw them and we started talking about them. While waiting in line for one of the more popular rides, we saw them coming. Their gimmick was saying they had friends at the front of the line and moved past everyone until they quietly settled in line somewhere close to the front. Well, again because of respect, I wasn't having it and I called them out. I rarely make scenes but to me, it was too disrespectful to just let it happen. Well, nothing came of it because the employee (also a teen) didn't throw them out. They just weaseled their way onto the ride and flipped us off as they started. My husband had involved himself, too.

CHAPTER 2: CONNECTION AND SHAME

Afterward, I asked my husband what value showed up for him in all that. He said fairness. I deeply value fairness but have made peace within myself that life is not fair. That doesn't rile me much. Yet, disrespect gets me activated. I feel every person deserves to be treated with respect, and even in that whole experience, I was trying to maintain a respectful approach. It was interesting because we were aligned in our actions to seek "justice" by kicking the kids out of the line, yet our motivation behind that behavior was different.

Another reason identifying core values is important is because when we are out of alignment with those values, we feel it. That visceral discomfort should be guilt if we can tolerate the way it feels without letting it morph into shame. We are often not living within our values. That is human. Yet, it is also a great ability as a human to recenter ourselves back into our integrity.

People often ask me, "How do you manage to be a therapist? Do you ever feel overwhelmed with all the stories and difficulties that people endure?" My answer is yes, at times I do feel saddened greatly by all the terrible things that happen in life. Still, it is far less than one would think because I feel so much hope. I believe with all my soul that growth is an integral part of life and people are capable of amazing change, even in the face of darkness and sorrow. I have seen it and will continue to see it throughout my life.

Sometimes the emotional pain gets worse before it gets better. That suffering is part of healing. When I was 18 months old, one of my older sisters was sick and wanted to drink some herbal tea to help her feel better. My mother heated some water in the microwave until it was boiling and left the mug on the low bar portion of the counter to cool before putting the tea bag in and giving it to my sister. As it cooled, she went into the other room. The low bar put the mug just at the right height for me, a curious little toddler, to grab and taste, as everything toddlers grab eventually ends up in their mouths. The water was so hot that it burned my tongue and scared me. That startled reaction caused me to spill the entire mug of boiling water onto my right arm.

At the time, I was wearing thermal full-body zip pajamas. That cotton material quickly absorbed the water. In pain, I held my arm close to my chest which, in turn, increased the heat of the water because of the thermal properties of the pajamas. My mother quickly responded to my cries. As she attempted to take my pajamas off, she realized that my skin had blistered so badly, it was pulled off with the sleeve. So they rushed me to the hospital where I was treated for third-degree burns. As with most burns, I was required to go to physical therapy every day for weeks to treat the skin and maintain mobility in my arm. Part of that treatment required me to be placed in a tin therapy tub of warm water while one of my parents held my arm. The physical therapist would debride my wound of dead skin.

The warm water and the poking and scraping of my skin caused terrible pain. I would scream and cry the entire time. It was the most horrific and traumatic experience I have ever lived through. Luckily, by the grace of God and the natural repression of memory that happens with trauma for children, I do not remember any of this. If it weren't for the large scar on my right arm and the stories I was told about the incident, I wouldn't even know anything happened. My parents, however, vividly remember. They essentially had to take their baby to a "torture chamber" every day and restrain her while the therapy commenced, unable to reassure me that the pain was for my own good. I was too young to understand that they were helping me.

I tell this story to clients often because when we are healing emotionally, things often get harder before they get better. The pain is part of the healing. Often that is because there is a "facing your demons" kind of experience. People have to be honest and accountable for what change needs to happen. That requires digging through the mire and experiencing a great deal of discomfort. Guilt helps us to be humble, vulnerable, accountable, and motivated toward change.

Dieter Uchtdorf, a well-known leader in the Church of Jesus Christ of Latter-Day Saints, said, "*Godly sorrow* leads to conversion and a change of heart. It causes us to hate sin and love goodness. It encourages us to stand up and walk in the light of Christ's love . . . heartfelt regret and true remorse for disobedience are often painful and very important steps in the sacred process of repentance. But when guilt leads to self-loathing or prevents us from rising again, it is impeding rather than promoting our repentance" (Uchtdorf, "You Can Do It Now!").

Repentance can have a lot of different meanings. For my purposes, it is not as much a process to "come clean" with God as it is a process of getting right with self. Some may feel those to be the same anyway.

Worldly Sorrow

The more I have read about shame in the scriptures, especially in the Old Testament, the more I see that there seems to be a horrible curse and misery associated with shame. Psalm 25:2 & 20 say, "Oh my God, I trust in thee, let me not be ashamed; let not mine enemies triumph over me," and, "Oh keep my soul, deliver me; let me not be ashamed; for I put my trust in thee." Any time shame is mentioned, it is coupled with great evil and suffering. Shame is an emotion and yet these descriptions and references make it out to be an experience comparable to hell.

In his book, "Living Buddha, Living Christ" well-known monk and author Tich Nhat Han states, "Jesus did not say that if you are angry with your brother, you will be put in a place called hell. He said that if you are angry with your brother, you are already in hell. Anger is hell." I am suggesting the same idea with shame. To be damned may not be a prison of fire and brimstone but a sentence of pure misery lived out in the mind. In *Paradise Lost,* John Milton wrote, "The mind is its place, and itself can make a heaven of hell, a hell of heaven…"

It is easy to understand how undesirable and miserable shame is. It makes us our own worst enemy, saying all the negative and critical things that a real enemy would say to break us down. What we don't always realize is how those degrading and damaging thoughts influence our actions and relationships. As a way to avoid feeling shame, we act, react, and interact poorly because shame feels crappy. Our instinct as humans is to move away from uncomfortable, crappy experiences. I feel this is a huge part of the struggle for most relationships.

In her book, *Daring Greatly*, Brené Brown gets into the extensive specifics of these poor behaviors that she found from her research. It is a great read about the individual behaviors she identified and the psychology behind them. My intent is not to rewrite her books, but I enthusiastically recommend that you read her works. We don't need a lot of explanation to understand that when we are struggling emotionally, we do not behave at our best. When I am stressed and anxious, I get impatient with my kids. I have less emotional capacity to be patient and kind. I listen less and yell more. Some examples of poor shame behavior are blaming, withdrawing, perfectionism, and clinging to others. I will address this more in Chapter 3. People also turn to addictions to avoid, or numb, the shame. I feel like addiction is one of shame's favorite flavors. Addiction and shame are tight.

What is missing from all the shame research is how it also makes us withdraw or distance ourselves from God. When we do not feel good enough, we assume that we must not be good enough for God. It's a funny thing because we pretend to hide from him which, of course, is not possible. We hide and distance ourselves and project our shame onto him. Anne Graham Lotz, the daughter of the famous evangelist Billy Graham, said, "If you feel far away from God right now, guess who moved?" (Lotz, *Magnificent Obsession*). This is the most dangerous part of shame. We turn away from God or Christ as a way to avoid our shame, but they are the best source to help us get through the shame.

This feeling of distance from God shows up a lot with other emotional struggles and disorders as well. I often hear clients who experience anxiety or depression talk about how they can't feel close to God. I call this "interference." When our emotions are so triggered and overwhelming, they get in the way of the peace and connection that we feel with God or the connection we could feel with ourselves. The connection is still there. The emotions are interfering with the "radio waves."

We can also be triggered into shame by our circumstances. Because our shame is individualized, so are our triggers. As I said before, when I am stressed, I am less patient with my kids. That becomes its own shame trigger because I feel bad about yelling and losing patience. In turn, I feel like a bad mom. Our shame and shame triggers are different at different stages of our lives. My shame as a teenager was triggered by two things: my body and boys. I was a dancer, which naturally brought up a lot of body image stuff. And also, by living and breathing as a straight, cisgender teenage girl, insecurities around boys developed.

CHAPTER 2: CONNECTION AND SHAME

Having awareness is the best first step toward dealing with shame. Awareness is the first step with any emotional change or healing. It is by recognizing where we fill in the blank of "I am not _____ enough" that we can observe our behaviors and assess how shame is overflowing into other parts of our lives. Sometimes awareness can even be the bulk of the solution. At times, we recognize triggers that we have no power to change. Being aware of the trigger releases some of the shame so we can manage the struggle better.

For me, my process of awareness created a big shift in my shame. I started learning about shame within a year of moving from Colorado to Idaho. In Colorado, there weren't as many people in my similar life situation. At that time, I was a devout Christian stay-at-home mother of three in my late twenties. In Colorado, that made me unique and I enjoyed being different. Most people my age in Colorado were still in college or grad school and far from marriage or kids. When I moved to Idaho, I moved into a sea of people like me. All young to middle-aged stay-at-home moms. And to top it off, they were all perfect-looking. I felt like every person around had their stuff together and was thriving. In my mind, everyone looked like me, except far better. I saw perfect-looking women with their perfect hair and perfectly-decorated houses and their perfectly-groomed children. They cooked perfect baked goods for church functions and had these adorable and elaborate birthday parties coupled with a theme, matching decorations, and party favors. I felt like my kids looked slightly homeless, my house was always in chaos, and when I came to church functions, I brought a family pack of Oreos.

For the first several months after the move, I felt depressed and disconnected. I felt like I couldn't keep up. Ironically though, I didn't want to look and act like everyone else. Blending in was not important to me. That conflict of emotions made my struggle even more confusing. I knew I shouldn't care. I knew that in my head but not in my heart. My heart felt that "not good enough" shame feeling. As I practiced more self-awareness, I looked at specific relationships that were my shame triggers. For a long time, I thought the "perfect-looking" people were my trigger. However, that theory was flawed because, over time, I had become friends with many of the "perfect-looking" people and didn't feel shame around them anymore. If anything, being around them helped kill my shame because I knew they were kind and loving people who completely accepted me, homeless-looking kids and all. Yet still, some relationships triggered my shame. I didn't understand it.

Then one day it hit me. I thought about these uncomfortable relationships. My shame wasn't being triggered by "perfect-looking" people, it was triggered by people that I couldn't connect with (who just so happened to also look perfect). These were people that, for whatever reason, were harder for me to get to know and feel close to. That lack of connection was my trigger.

I saw this struggle with some family members. I saw myself as hugely flawed in comparison. I hyper-focused on the differences we had in interests, fashion, and talents, thinking that was my struggle. In reality, it was our lack of connection that made me uneasy. Connection is cultivated when you feel safe and accepted by a person—when you can open up to them and be vulnerable. I didn't feel safe being myself with this family member. Once I realized that connection was the issue, my perspective changed. I saw my family differently and saw myself differently.

This process of understanding shame does something really neat. It is more than just understanding ourselves and how our shame works. It is understanding how shame shows up for others. We see it in ourselves and everyone else around us, and it changes everything. There can be a higher capacity for understanding, empathy, and patience when we realize what emotions are underneath poor behaviors. People aren't just selfish or arrogant or shy or angry. People are just people. Their emotions influence their behavior which manifests as selfish or arrogant, shy or angry.

I tell clients, "Observe your shame. Find out where it lives and who it hangs out with." Diving into my shame created a whole new worldview. It helped me to separate the deep-seated shame and my small social insecurities. Now, I may feel a little self-conscious around really "perfect-looking" people, but that doesn't make me feel shame. I still feel solid in my worth. Most days, I like that I'm not perfect. I try to embrace it. But when I have a relationship with someone whom I cannot connect with, I don't feel safe being myself. I know my shame will show up, but that solely resides in me. My shame would tell me

CHAPTER 2: CONNECTION AND SHAME

I'm not as good as they are. That shame is a lie. I am as valuable as anyone else. I just don't feel comfortable around them. It's possible they don't feel comfortable around me either. Understanding that separation helped me to focus more on the individual in the relationship. It became more about understanding them instead of feeling stuck in my shame. Compassion is a special thing. Not only does it bring us together as humans, but it also heals us.

We see examples of shame and poor reactions to shame all over the scriptures. The Pharisees were in constant competition with each other over who was more righteous, more knowledgeable, or who was best at "debunking" Christ's teachings. Luke 11: 53–54 says, "The scribes and the Pharisees began to urge him vehemently, and to provoke him to speak of many things: laying wait for him, and seeking to catch something out of his mouth, that they might accuse him." They spent so much energy trying to prove themselves right and disprove others. People who work hardest to prove their worth or confidence are the ones who struggle the most with believing they have worth. People solid in their own worth and value don't waste time trying to prove anything. They already know it. No doubt the Pharisees were contending with a lot of personal shame. Psychologist Maxwell Maltz wrote, "An inferiority complex and superiority complex are merely opposite sides of the same coin" (Maltz, Kennedy, and Maltz, *The New Psycho-Cybernetics*).

Shame is best friends with depression. Anxiety, too. Some of the lowest and most torturous emotional experiences we can have as humans are caused by shame and depression. So low that an unfortunate number of people take their own lives in an attempt to escape the pain. People who have been in those low, depressed places often say, "I'm just so tired." The toll depression takes is far more than emotional. The body, mind, and spirit are all assaulted. For many, this despair infiltrates their relationship with God. They see His love as conditional.

For years, I had worked as a part-time therapist at a university counseling center. It was an ideal job for years. I could set my hours, which helped me balance my profession with raising my four young children. Throughout that time, I knew that I eventually would want to go full-time. It was just a matter of timing. I had a lot of good support from my boss and coworkers. After about six years, I felt ready to apply for the next full-time opening. This was met with a lot of enthusiastic responses from the office. To give some reference, I had mentioned it to my boss and after a weekly staff meeting with all the full-time people, he mentioned my interest. I got four calls that day from people in that meeting excited for me to apply and eager to support me. That felt so good! Up to this point, my interaction with the office was fairly minimal. I usually went into my generic office space shared by all part-timers, worked my sessions, and went home. So to have any positive interactions, not to mention highly enthusiastic interactions, was a big boost.

It is important to know that another shame trigger of mine is colleagues. It was hard for me to hold my head up with confidence around people who had twenty-plus years of experience. I knew my clients liked me and benefited from our sessions, but my shame still told me I wasn't "experienced or smart enough." In the field of mental health therapy, there are oceans of science, research, and different clinical methods to understand and master. I rarely felt like I'd learned enough. So there I was, ready to enter into a new realm professionally, and I was finally getting validation from my peers. I was high on it. At the same time, I was trying to stay rational and remember that I was only ready to apply. I was not hired yet. But hearing things like, "You are a shoo-in," and "Why wouldn't you be hired?" made it hard not to get my hopes up.

So I applied, waited several weeks, interviewed, and waited some more. I was one of the two final candidates and was waiting seven anxiety-ridden days for the call. It finally came on the 4th of July. I was on a big family outing with my husband, kids, and lots of his family. I didn't get the job. As much as I tried to stay neutral in my expectations, I failed. That was a massive blow on many levels, mostly because I was hungry for more validation. My young "inner therapist child" just wanted to hear she was good enough.

The blows just kept on coming. All of this happened right at the peak of Covid-19. My part-time job with the office was dropped temporarily because the college students were all forced to go home and complete classes online. My best option was to go into private practice. This was not something I had ever planned on. With private

CHAPTER 2: CONNECTION AND SHAME

practice, there is all the work of setting up a small business as well as a hell of a lot of work getting credentialed with any insurance company you want to work with (each company has a different approval process).

So I started all the work. After weeks of applications and phone calls, I found out most insurance companies wouldn't accept me unless I finished another level of clinical licensing. That was a process I could have finished years earlier, but it wasn't a requirement with the university. The process also required a supervisor. I had a supervisor on campus. Once I went into private practice though, she no longer felt comfortable working with me because of the liability. I lost her, too.

So to summarize: I didn't get the job, lost my old job, couldn't work with most insurance companies, and lost my supervisor. The icing on the cake was, during this same time frame, I got an email from a big publisher rejecting this book. I was at my lowest point. My anxiety and stress were so high that I hardly ate or slept. And as incredibly supportive as my husband had been throughout all this, my marriage was taking a hit. I got close to throwing in the towel.

Every five minutes my shame was telling me I was a big failure. If I had been hungry for professional validation before, now I was starving. I had a choice. I was very familiar with the concept of failure from helping clients. I knew how to cope and treat my shame. I could get swallowed up by the overpowering volume of "you're not enough," or I could fight it. So I kept going. I practiced better self-compassion and lots of self-care. I meditated more. I also talked and talked and accepted the love and empathy around me. I could feel the power that shame had. I could also feel the power of my infinite worth. I believed that every human in this world was valuable and I was no exception. God created us all equal in worth. I knew that and needed to lean into that belief with extra gusto.

One of my very favorite quotes explaining God's, abundant love is, "Heavenly Father loves you—each of you. That love never changes. It is not influenced by your appearance, your possessions, or the amount of money in your bank account. It is not changed by your talents or abilities. It is simply there. It is there for you when you are sad or happy, discouraged or hopeful. God's love is there whether or not you feel you deserve love. It is simply always there" (Monson, "We Never Walk Alone"). Our shame can keep us from connecting with others and with God. We have to challenge that shame. We have to believe that we are worth fighting for. We have to look at ourselves as God does.

In the end, I was able to find a way through my struggles. Some things took longer than others. Within four months, I had a full calendar of clients and within a year, I had completed all the state requirements for my clinical license. The best part of all was that I learned to validate myself as a professional which, in turn, minimized my shame around that. Now I can confidently admit what I know and what I don't know without the inner dread of shame. I have learned how to love that little "inner therapist child." She's kind of great.

Practice

When it comes to understanding shame for any individual, I always start with self-awareness. Try to answer these questions without placing any judgment on the responses. Objective observation of self is the best first step. Don't try to change or evaluate it. Just observe. If you were a scientist assigned to observe a species of monkeys in the jungle, you watch and gather data without any judgment or effort to change the monkeys. Change comes later.

- Where does shame show up for you?

- How does your shame fill in the blank? "I am not _____ enough." (*There may be multiple answers.*)

- Where do you feel it in your body?

- What people, places, or experiences trigger shame?

- What people, places, or experiences calm the shame? (*These are important things to note. You want to be around these people or be doing these things more often.*)

CHAPTER 3

Shame

As adults, we recognize shame far better than we did as kids. Children and teens have a limited emotional vocabulary which hinders their ability to understand themselves. However, it does not hinder their ability to feel and experience emotion. An unfortunate truth for many children is that their shame is given to them through dialogue from family or friends. Whether it is verbal or implied, intentional or not, the idea that "you are not enough" can start very young and come from the very people who are supposed to instill confidence and joy.

I have heard a disappointing number of stories about things parents told their children that were shaming and degrading. Those damaging words slowly became truth and, after so long, they become the words that the children tell themselves. Shaming voices reincarnated as personal shame. I talked about Stacy in the last chapter. Her shame was disguised as her mother's. The shame voice was completely Stacy's. The same thing can happen with siblings, bullies, teachers, and friends. At some point, we hear shaming things about ourselves, and then we believe them.

Narrative therapy is a popular method in psychology that focuses on the stories we tell ourselves about our lives. Shame gets into that process and disrupts the objective perspective of our stories. This is something that can be easily identified among siblings. Take two siblings, brother and sister, both given similar treatment from parents, similar opportunities and experiences, and similar competencies. Into adulthood, we find the brother sibling faring well emotionally and maintaining healthy relationships. The sister is not. She is deep in shame and struggles, and her relationships are suffering significantly. What is the difference? Is one person just more resilient, happy, or emotionally capable than the other? There may be some truth to that. Some people are naturally happier, but joy comes with the practice of certain skills. At some point, the sister started to tell herself a certain story that grew in volume. "My parents love my brother more." "I will never be as good as him." "Everything I do is a screw-up."

That story creates a certain lens (just like the shades of sunglasses) that changes her perspective on her entire life. She could see her parents praising her brother for good grades. Even though they also praised her for good grades, because of the skewed lens, she only saw the praise of her brother, which fueled the shame. Before long, she is seeing everything as negative feedback and her shame is devouring it all.

Now let's consider the brother. In reality, he was no more favored by his parents or experiences. He would see praise and success happen to his sister and others. This did not influence his narrative. He still experienced shame, like all people, but he also exercised more rational thinking. He saw his parents put a lot of effort into helping his sister feel better. They would, at times, give her more time and attention because of it. He saw that as something parents do when their kid is struggling. He did not let that start a narrative that they loved her more than him.

The great thing about narratives is that by becoming more mature and self-aware, we can rewrite our stories. One way I do that in session is with an exercise called the "empty chair." This is a method popularized through the Gestalt psychology theory. I have tailored this method a little to fit my therapeutic style. It is one of my favorite tools because it can evoke a lot of powerful and important emotions. I use it as a way to start to rewrite the narrative that started during childhood.

First, I pull an empty chair over and place it in front of where the client is sitting. Before even acknowledging the chair, I ask the client to think of a time when they started to feel different about themselves, or when the shame started. I explain that when we are born into this world, we do not feel shame. As small toddlers, we have "no shame." Nothing is embarrassing. We can wear or say anything we want without fear of judgment. It is the only time we can wear clothes backward, have food stuck in our teeth, say something offensive, and pass a little gas without caring about it! Somewhere between then and adulthood, that all changes. We feel pressure to act, talk, or perform in certain ways to be good enough. Most people can think of a specific age or period of time. Some may even have an isolated experience. I have them tell me more about that age or time and what was happening. I ask for more specific events and specific emotions.

This is usually something I do after we have had some discussion about shame, so we can use those terms to frame the experiences talked about. After we identify a time, I tell them that child is sitting in the empty chair. I'll say, "Seven-year-old Ben is sitting right there." Many times that shift is emotional. I am helping the client see their younger, more innocent self, whom they know but have never taken time to meet. I ask, "What does he look like? What is he wearing? What does his hair look like?" This helps create a very specific picture for both of us.

Next, I ask, "How does he feel?" This takes the experience deeper. The client verbalizes the pain while placing it on "another" person they have started to feel compassion for. Then, to take it all the way, I say, "What did that little boy need to hear from someone then that would have helped him feel better? Tell him that." The client starts to talk to the younger self and begins to rewrite those negative stories. There is a lot to learn and understand about the psychology of this experience. Suffice it to say, the majority of clients who do this with me feel significant shifting. They begin to challenge the lies their shame told them as children. As a side note, this method doesn't always work with the same power for all people. There are a fair amount of people who, for various reasons, are unable to feel and harness that compassion. They can still rewrite their story and foster self-compassion in other ways.

There are many behaviors we naturally engage in that feed our shame. The most common behaviors are

1. Comparison
2. Self-criticism
3. Over-valuing other people's opinions

We all engage in these behaviors to some degree. Not all of that is bad. Comparing ourselves in a healthy small dose can help us be socially aware and conscious of healthy ways to interact. That small amount of comparison is not unlike objective observation. It doesn't have to lead to judgment or shame. If our criticism is a constructive and honest self-evaluation, we can become more motivated to change undesirable characteristics. It could be argued that healthy self-criticism is important for self-awareness and accountability. Also, when we have an appropriate amount of care for other people, it allows us to be more considerate and conscious of other people and their feelings. There is merit in wanting other people to feel comfortable or happy. The ultimate problem is being able to engage in these behaviors in a rational way that does not lead to shame. That is hard. The line separating healthy and rational from unhealthy and shameful is thin. Most of us kind of suck at this. It's like when you buy a bag of chips and you're only supposed to eat one. Sure, it's possible, but very few people manage to do it.

Comparison

I want you to pay attention to how your body and heart feel when you think of the word comparison. It immediately makes my skin crawl. I feel the tension in my neck and shoulders. I start to notice a slightly nauseous feeling. There's a heaviness in my heart. I guarantee that I am not the only one with a physical shame reaction to comparison. In our society today, there is ample opportunity to compare ourselves not only to everyone around us but to everyone in the world. Social media has transformed how we view each other and has changed the way we view ourselves. Not only do teenage kids have to worry about fitting in at school, they worry about likes, comments, followers, and what filter to use. It takes comparison to the Olympic level. Many years ago, when I first started using Facebook, it was really exciting. I was reconnecting with old friends and seeing where their lives had taken them. I had been out of high school for seven or eight years, so a lot had changed among my friends.

As time went on, I was essentially done with the "catching up" phase of Facebook. My interest in it changed and so did my experience with it. I found myself feeling cruddy when I logged off. The comparisons were making me sick. I found myself ruminating about certain posts or people and thinking about their lives, or adventures, for hours after getting off. That caused a struggle that would infiltrate my day. So I tried to combat this by posting "real" posts. I posted pictures of my house when it was torn apart by kids, or my closet (which never looked good). I shared my struggle with nursing my fourth baby and how I couldn't produce enough milk to get past three months (that was a huge shame trigger). I was trying to be vulnerable and more open as a way to cut through all the "picture-perfect" posts.

I was trying to balance out all the incomplete facades that seemed to be all anyone posted. However, I still felt down every time I was on Facebook so I decided to quit. If I couldn't change my experience of the activity, I was going to stop the activity. It helped so much and I haven't missed it one bit. I joke that I "broke up" with Facebook. "He was always making me feel bad about myself and was always checking out other girls. It was a toxic relationship. I don't miss him at all." Initially, I thought I would miss keeping up with some friends. It turned out that type of connection was mostly synthetic anyway. For the people I cared about, I would keep in touch in other ways.

We can't always remove the opportunity to compare but we can make significant changes to experience it less. Adjustment in relationships, behaviors, or hobbies can help us focus on our intrinsic value rather than on other people's superficial displays. Roosevelt said that "comparison is the thief of joy." When we sit with our eyes perfectly fixed on others, we will never see our own beauty and strength.

I think there are developmental phases throughout life when it comes to comparison. There is something about getting older and learning that all of us are struggling with something. Comparison is futile. It is never a fair comparison because every person is so different, with a different life. Given the sheer volume of life's details, there is no accurate measurement from one person to another. Life is the only effective teacher. As much as I preach that we shouldn't compare, I'm sure I will know far more when I'm in my eighties than I do now in my late thirties.

Self-Criticism

Any form it takes, whether it is an idea that we hear and adopt for ourselves or something we pick up from experiences along the way, self-criticism packs a huge punch. That punch is usually delivered through thousands of small pokes. A person might say, "I'm sorry. I don't know what I was thinking. I'm so dumb sometimes." That takes a small personal jab at themselves. That comment probably doesn't linger or even sting. But when we say things like that to ourselves over and over again, it adds up and becomes our truth. That being said, remarks like that aren't causing new shame. They are evidence of existing shame. The continued cutting thoughts maintain shame like a simmering pot of soup that needs the occasional stir to make sure everything is well-blended.

It is interesting to see what God tells Moses and Enoch when they were expressing their inadequacy to Him. In Exodus 4:11-12, God says to Moses, "Who hath made man's mouth? or who maketh the dumb, or deaf, or the seeing, or the blind? have not I the Lord? Now therefore go, and I will be with thy mouth, and teach thee what thou shalt say."

God gives these men an immense charge to be faithful and know that He will create a path for them to fulfill their callings. We often do that in various "callings" in our lives, whether it be our jobs, roles in families, or other meaningful responsibilities. We cut ourselves down. Our shame convinces us that it is by our works alone that our callings will be completed and we will fall short.

If you think about the divisiveness of criticism, you can recognize how damaging it is to potential. It can be motivating, like the critical coach who uses threats to get athletes to perform. That motivation only produces fear-based performances. The coach who encourages and gives direct but supportive feedback allows for the athlete to step into their capacity and thrive. This concept can be spiritual. Connecting with yourself in a way that is so honest and hopeful that you can push to new levels of achievement, understanding, and experience. If that is not a divine experience, I don't know what is.

One of my favorite shows on PBS is *Call the Midwife*. Honestly, it is the only show I feel absolutely no guilt or shame about watching when a new season comes out and I binge nonstop. (Not to say I don't binge on other shows, but I usually feel bad about it.) This show depicts the lives of midwives and midwifery nuns working together in the East End of London during the 1950s and 60s. One of the nuns, Sister Monica Joan, said, "Often we find the hands of God at the end of our own arms." When we are empowered to be our best selves and chase the afterlife, we find God.

Criticizing and demeaning ourselves degrades a divine creation, a person with immense capacity and potential. The opposite of doubt is belief. Believing in ourselves enlists the virtue of God within us. Encouraging and supporting ourselves, especially when we mess up and struggle, allow the power of God to pull us through.

OVERVALUING OTHERS' OPINIONS

Another link in the shame struggle is caring too much about what other people think. The biggest flaw is that we're usually wrong in our assumption of what they think. David Foster Wallace, a well-known novelist, said, "You will become way less concerned about what other people think of you when you realize how seldom they do" (Wallace and Bissell, *Infinite Jest*). Part of this misperception is projection. We easily assume that everyone else is thinking, seeing, and judging us. A common theme I hear when working with social anxieties is, "I am always worried I will say something wrong." Those clients are immediately assuming that if they say something out of the ordinary or stumble over their words, other people will judge them. I know plenty of people, myself at the top of the list, who "say something wrong," but it isn't a big deal to other people. Good people are quite forgiving, and most of us are good people.

Again, social media and our current methods of interaction are not helping us. Talking through screens gives us the time to craft a perfect response. We type, read, reread, and sometimes even have a friend analyze it before we push send. The word craft is important because written words can be easily misinterpreted. However, it is different from real people. We have a ton more communication feedback when we talk face to face. We shouldn't feel the pressure to be perfect in our conversations. That takes away authenticity.

The concern about what other people think goes beyond the conversation. In truth, we have a lot of evidential support because some people *are* judgmental. I am most insecure around family or friends who I hear talking bad about other people because who's to say they don't talk about me that same way? The suffocating pressure to act perfectly so people won't judge isn't worth the pain and anxiety. Judgments happen, yet they happen less often than we think. That fear keeps us from truly participating in our relationships. As we know, true connection is forged through vulnerability. Vulnerability cannot happen unless we free ourselves from the bondage created out of the fear of what others think.

The Shame Trigger

It is important to know that when it comes to serious mental health issues, shame resilience work is not a complete treatment. I use it in conjunction with many other treatment methods. Methods which I won't get into here because there are libraries full of content on mental health treatment. The ideas I am suggesting here are not to replace but add to existing resources and methods. Shame, as well as anxiety, trauma, stress, depression, and other mental health problems, trigger the brain's stress response in similar ways.

Perhaps the most helpful brain science for people to understand is that of the stress response. Biologically, our brains are wired in ways to help us function and survive. One way our brains do that is through our nervous system. Here is a classic example I use with most clients:

Let's say I wake up in my bed and find that my house is on fire. Instantly, my body and brain receive all sorts of information communicating there is a real threat. I smell the smoke. I see the flames. I feel the heat. In that same moment, my body will choose to fight, flight, freeze, submit, or attach (submit being shame, and attach means needing other people to regulate overwhelming emotions). In a house fire, I will probably choose "flight" or run. In the back part of the brain (amygdala and hippocampus), my nervous system will be triggered and kick into high gear. My eyes will dilate. Adrenaline will pump into my system. My muscles will be tense and ready to move.

At the same time, the parasympathetic nervous system deactivates because my body is trying to prioritize the functions of my body that are needed most. This means my digestive system shuts down, I stop growing hair and regulating my body temperature, and, most importantly, the front part of my brain (the prefrontal cortex/logic center) shuts down, too. I don't need to be thinking; I just need to be surviving.

In an actual dangerous situation, this physical response in our body is important to help keep us alive. We see this in wildlife all the time. Bears fight, deer flee, and possums freeze. However, there are several problems for humans. The first is that our brains misinterpret many things as threats that are not like relationships, work, school, and other big stressors. The second problem is that when we are triggered, because we lose the full function of the prefrontal cortex, we can't think rationally. We feel stressed and panicky and can't think through the reality of the situation. We are safe but our brains can't process that we are safe.

This triggering response especially shows up in people who have experienced significant trauma or abuse. We all experience it to some degree. Research shows that most people are operating in the sympathetic nervous system far more than in the parasympathetic nervous system. That's because we are all so stressed out! However, understanding all of this helps us to take better steps to manage our triggers. Over time, people can feel less triggered and the body and brain can better interpret threats.

Another interesting part of this research is that two other stress responses are often overlooked. We have the classic fight, flight, and freeze. We also have submit and attach. These are responses that show up in relationships. Submit is what shame looks like in action. Submit is the dog that cowers with its tail between its legs because it fears abuse. Submit is when the rape victim just allows the rape to happen because her body knows there will be less pain. Submit is when we make ourselves small physically or emotionally, just to survive. Attach is when a person clings to another to feel safe and stable.

For those who have experienced trauma and abuse, there is help that specifically focuses on triggers and "rewiring" the brain. If you, or someone you know, is seriously struggling with a mental health disorder, it's best to seek professional help. This book is a good resource for mending emotional wounds, but it is not a complete guide for those with significant issues.

PRACTICE

When it comes to shame awareness, sometimes it can be overwhelming, especially if you see shame show up frequently and in many places. Sometimes that can become too overwhelming and multiply the shame. Be careful and pace yourself. It is important to be self-aware and take breaks. Go at a manageable pace. Some people may not be able to go at it alone. Professionals can help with this process as needed.

- When was a time in your childhood that shame started to show up? Do you have a vivid memory of feeling shame as a child?

  ◦ How old were you?

  ◦ What was going on in your life at that time?

  ◦ What did you look like?

  ◦ How would an onlooker have thought about how you felt? What did you feel?

  ◦ Write a letter to that child and say the things that no one was saying to you, those things that could have helped. (*Be open to ideas and emotions this might bring up. Resist pushing back your feelings. Also, if this is too hard and you have nothing to say, be aware of why it is difficult. Be curious about why you can't talk or say anything positive to that child.*)

CHAPTER 3: SHAME

—Include in the letter how you (as an adult) feel about this child.

—Do you care? Why or why not?

—If possible, talk to that child about why their shame is a lie.

- When do you struggle with comparison the most?

- About the quote above, "Comparison is the thief of joy," how does comparison steal away your joy?

- If your son/daughter struggled with comparison in the same way you do (real or imagined), what would you say or do to help?

CHAPTER 4

Deflecting Shame

WHENEVER MY KIDS ASKED IF SANTA IS REAL, MY GO-TO WAS, "WELL, what do you think? Do you think Santa is real?" The classic deflection tactic by answering a question with a question. Politicians do it all the time. This is the best way to avoid giving a direct and honest answer. We use deflecting as a tactic with our shame as well. Psychologists have many names for this deflecting behavior. I will call them shame deflectors. These deflectors provide ideal opportunities to sidestep the shame and place attention elsewhere. However, this doesn't address the shame at all, it just minimizes it momentarily. The most common examples of these are:

- Perfectionism
- Blame
- Judgment
- Withdrawal
- People-pleasing
- Addictions

Perfectionism is an extremely big problem. So much so that I have devoted all of Chapter 5 to it. I feel like this is something especially common in religious cultures. There is a lot of emphasis on being righteous or choosing God's way. The problem with that messaging is that it doesn't allow much room to be human, especially when the standard is Jesus or God. That creates rigid behaviors and standards for self that are overwhelming.

Blaming does most of its work inside our heads. Such blaming thought patterns have a strong influence on how we feel about ourselves and others. I recognized this behavior in myself when I was cleaning out the freezer in my garage. Months earlier, a jar of frozen jam that was on the door rack leaked all over the freezer. As I was cleaning it, I realized that nearly half of the jar must have leaked out and seeped under the bottom of the freezer. I had to remove a plastic cover to clean it. After scraping the raspberry goo for the better part of an hour, I remembered my previous reactions to the mess. Every time I opened the freezer, I would curse the jam. There was sticky stuff all over things in the freezer and I just hated opening that door. More specifically, I was blaming my mother-in-law for giving it to me. "Why does she always give us so much jam? Now it's covering everything with sticky gunk!" "There are jars and jars of this stuff and we don't even eat it." I was blaming her, my wonderful mother-in-law, for giving us delicious freezer jam.

As I was cleaning, I realized I was blaming her to avoid my shame. Every time I opened that freezer, I was reminded that I had not cleaned up the mess. Every time I opened the freezer, I was immediately reminded of yet one more thing on my long to-do list that I wasn't getting done. So, as a way to avoid the discomfort of my own emotions, I blamed my mother-in-law. Let it also be known that we love her jam. My kids only want to eat her jam. We didn't eat it because I forgot it was in there, as I do with half the food I put in the freezer (another shame trigger). "I am lazy and unorganized. I can't even keep track of the food in my freezer. I just keep buying more without taking inventory of what I already have."

The blaming was a deflection mixed with horribly irrational thinking. Who blames a kind, wonderful woman for giving them jam just because it made a mess? Irrational thinking is always part of the shame experience. Again, this is because it is a stress response and the prefrontal cortex is less functional.

Not everyone ascribes to the story of Adam and Eve. It provides a good example of blame. After Adam and Eve partook of the forbidden fruit, God found them hiding in the garden. Adam was quick to place the blame on Eve as the reason for his transgression. Eve quickly shifted the blame to Satan. Now, in reality, some people are deserving of blame. Satan is probably at the top of the list. The problem with blame is not about the question of whether or not another person deserves it. Blame puts the blamers in a disconnected state with themselves. They put all their energy into blaming other people whom they cannot control or change. That puts blamers in a no-win situation, which causes a lot of anger. Anger is a first-level emotion. Underneath it, you can almost always find shame. There is a great freeing experience when you can let go of blame. That may or may not be the same thing as forgiveness; rather, it is letting go of the need to place fault.

In marriage, blaming puts each spouse in a corner waiting for the other person to change. There is no path to resolution. The better way is to focus on oneself and see what part of the struggle to own. When there is hurt, we need to express pain and try to explain why we feel that way. For instance, my husband feels a lot of frustration when we are spending time together after the kids go to bed and I'm busy on my phone.

There are two ways he could communicate his frustration to me: "I hate when you are on your phone so much. Why can't you just stop?" Or, he could say, "When you are on your phone during our limited time together, I feel like you don't value me and don't value spending time with me. It makes me feel disconnected from you. It triggers my shame and makes me feel like I am not enough." The first example would make it very easy for me to be defensive and fight back. "I have been going all day and finally have time to catch up on some messages. Don't get mad at me for something you do all the time." (Fighting blame with more blame.) Or, "Someone texted me and I can't ignore it. That would be rude. Do you want me to be rude?" The second possible reaction invites empathy and understanding. He is expressing his shame and desire to be close to me. There is no blame in that approach. He focuses on his own emotions.

When my kids were younger, bedtime was the best example of this. I loathed bedtime. I'd get anxious leading up to it every night. There's something fantastically designed about bedtime with multiple little kids to make it so hard to get them to bed. In our family, we had a fairly strict bedtime routine during the school year. At 7:00, all the kids were supposed to clean their rooms, get into their pajamas, and brush their teeth. Then they all read or were read to, for a certain amount of time. We finished with family prayer. That process was never smooth. It was filled with a lot of telling kids to brush their teeth, start reading, get back in their rooms, change into pajamas, stop licking each other, stop dancing on the table, take the dog out of the cupboard, and don't spray water all over the place. Once they were finally done and in bed, that wasn't the end of it. We had to tuck in the kids and re-tuck in the kids as they inevitably got out of bed for water or complained that they couldn't fall asleep after three minutes. Then there was my personal favorite—the random question they had to ask immediately even though it had nothing to do with anything, like, "Mom . . . um . . . well . . . uh . . . what day is it today?" That was my four-year-old's go-to.

My husband often used the first phase of bedtime, the cleanup, as downtime and would read, check his phone, or play the guitar. I was stuck in the war zone, cleaning and nagging the children to clean. Just as he gets highly set off when I'm on my phone, I go bonkers, irritated that he sits while I'm running all over wrangling kids (like herding cats). To me, it felt like he didn't care about helping me and was making me do all the dirty work. I hated that part of the day, and when I felt left to do it on my own, it was infuriating. Now, I make my dear husband out to be lazy and completely inconsiderate. That's not him at all. He just had a very different approach to bedtime. He viewed it as something the kids need to do without "helicoptering." He felt we should give them a time frame to get their responsibilities completed. If they didn't finish in time, we should enforce consequences. In theory, I agreed with his method. In reality, the kids were never really cleaning or brushing teeth or reading as well as I needed them to, so I would jump in to help (also known as micromanaging). I wanted to finally be done with bedtime. Neither way is completely right or completely wrong.

I could communicate my emotions in one of two ways. I could blame: "Brady, help us out. Don't just sit there and play your guitar. Good gracious, this is not chill time." Or, I could speak my emotions: "Brady, when you are not engaging with me and the kids during this time, it makes me feel like you don't care to help. On a deeper level, it makes me feel like you don't care about me because I am trying so hard. I get impatient and frustrated with the kids and I need your help. Then I could be more pleasant and we could get it all done together." I have used a combination of those approaches several times and always get a better response with the latter. By communicating my feelings, I am inviting him to help because I need it.

Judgment. Some think that judgment and blame are the same things; however, they are different behaviors from a similar source. Blame is placing responsibility or fault onto someone else. Judgment places a distinct evaluation of something or someone as good or bad (usually bad). There is always judgment with blame but not always blame with judgment. We all judge to some degree. Some people take it so far that their entire worldview is tainted by a constant negative evaluation of others. For these people, a hefty dose of judgment causes them to focus on the faults of others so they don't have to judge themselves. It has been said in many different ways; we often judge in others what we judge in ourselves.

Take the image of the meanest girl you can imagine. Let's take the Hollywood stereotype. She's popular and has a posse of girls around her. She is very attractive. Looks are so important to her that she only engages in activities or events that are socially popular. She doesn't like to do anything different or unique. She focuses her efforts on teasing others about their looks and for not fitting in. Maybe she picks on the harp-playing girl with glasses and braces who loves playing long, interactive board games. In reality, the mean girl is working hard every day to convince herself and everyone around her that she is better than the harp player. She has to prove that she is pretty and popular. She has to prove it because underneath it all, she's terrified that she isn't those things. She bullies others around her because it keeps her away from her shame and builds a false sense of importance. That fallacy takes a lot of maintenance and convincing. The more energy put into proving, the more severe the insecurity.

The bully is an extreme example of this behavior. I see some of this behavior, usually from clients' past experiences. I evaluate their level of judgment by assessing their expectations of other people.

To build self-compassion, I often ask, "Would you talk to another person the way you talk to yourself?" The common answer is "no." Occasionally it is "yes." Sometimes expectations of self and others are rigid, without flexibility. There is little option to be different or feel differently. It is so frustrating when they believe everyone should act and react a certain way. They're constantly battling to get others to do things differently. In some cases, these individuals have personality disorders that contribute to the rigidity of their worldview. When a person is judgmental of others, their self-critic is even more insufferable. There is no escape from self-judgment. It becomes an impossible task to "be good enough."

Withdrawal and **people-pleasing** are at opposite ends of the same rope. Some of that has to do with personality traits. An introvert is likely to withdraw when they feel shame—that's their default setting. However, that doesn't mean only introverts withdraw. John and Julie Gottman are two of the leading clinical researchers in the field of couples therapy. They have defined the "Four Horsemen of the Apocalypse," which are the behaviors that show up in a partnership that are most dangerous to the relationship. These behaviors are criticism, contempt, defensiveness, and stonewalling. Each one is similar to the shame deflectors.

This is where withdrawal shows up for me. I am, in most situations, an extrovert. So withdrawing is not something I do often. Yet in my marriage, when my husband and I are having a difficult conversation or arguing, it often triggers my shame and I withdraw. It starts with a numb feeling that builds up. I feel heavy and don't want to talk anymore. I feel myself becoming less engaged and wanting to be alone. This is also my stress response in other relationships. Withdrawal is a form of freezing. As I have become more self-aware, I can recognize when this is happening. If I am communicating well, I might say something like, "I'm feeling triggered," or "My brain is offline and I'm not receiving any information. I need to take some time to self-soothe. I promise I'll come back to this when I'm in a better place." Always promise and commit to return to the conversation.

People-pleasing is exactly what it sounds like—attempting to avoid any discomfort by putting effort into pleasing others. This behavior believes, "If I do all I can to make sure they like/approve/love me, then it will all be okay and I won't feel bad about myself anymore." Since the desire to please others comes from shame, it's not sincere. It's a way of trying to gain approval for reassurance. Conscious or not, it's a manipulative tactic because they can't tolerate the discomfort of others. They do all they can to keep others happy and avoid personal discomfort. I've met several people who are good at saying, "I don't care, what do you want to do?" They can't answer for themselves, express their own opinion, or say what they want to do. They lose their sense of self and individuality.

One client, Jenny, was a mild, easy-going person. Others enjoyed being around her because she had a very calming effect. Her people-pleasing style was not so "in your face." It was subtle and often went unnoticed. However, she had lived her whole life trying to satisfy those around her. Much of this stemmed from her family dynamic. It was magnified through other life experiences and her general selfless nature. As long as she could keep everyone happy, she could also be happy. In addition, she felt uncomfortable thinking about herself. Thinking about others kept her comfortable. If she thought about herself, she felt shame.

This people-pleasing behavior was her safe zone. However, after years and years of this, she had no relationship with herself. She was the last person she was interested in. She also was an extreme overachiever. She felt like she had to spend all of her time either serving or taking care of others, or diving into the many classes and extracurricular activities she was involved in. There was no downtime to be with herself. She was also a good athlete. There were several times she got injured but kept pushing it, ignoring the injury, or telling people she didn't want to be a burden. Jenny was sacrificing her body for the perceived comfort of other people.

It is good to care about other people and desire to serve. I am not discrediting Jenny's good heart. But we must not lose ourselves in the process. Christ was the most important example of service. He also valued his worth and needs. He maintained his sense of self and self-respect. That allowed him to serve better. We love others better when we love ourselves.

Addiction is what Brené calls a numbing behavior. This means that people turn to addiction to avoid feeling shame or any other emotional discomfort. It is easier to numb the pain. Just as numbing is a method used in medicine to manage pain, it is temporary and eventually wears off. That's what feeds the addiction cycle. People feel pain, and they turn to addiction to numb the pain. The numbness wears off and the pain hits again, sometimes harder. So people turn back to the addiction, sometimes more intensely. They lose their ability to tolerate pain and discomfort. Those who can tolerate discomfort well are more resilient.

Addictions come in many shapes and sizes. All addictions are numbing but not all numbing behaviors are addictions. The diagnosis of addiction is when a behavior(s) interferes with an individual's ability to function normally. They cannot stop when they want, despite negative consequences. Many of us numb our pain but are not addicted. Still, that doesn't make numbing an acceptable behavior.

I numb with Netflix or Hulu or whatever streaming service is carrying my newest binge. When I have a lot going on and my to-do list is hefty, I check out. I want to stop thinking about all the things and just watch my favorite psychological thriller, British mystery, or medical drama. I want to push a pause button on my brain and push play on my computer. At the moment, it is nice and I feel better. I'm avoiding the stress and anxiety. But the watching inevitably ends and I have to return to life. I have less time to get things done. Even worse, when I am numbing with shows, I am not engaging with people I love and value. I unintentionally (or sometimes intentionally) ignore or avoid them so I can keep numbing. Not okay.

Sometimes activities can look numbing at face value, but for that individual, they are therapeutic. This requires a really honest evaluation of self to identify what is numbing and what is therapeutic. Another way to look at it is to determine what is self-care and what is selfishness. Sometimes it could be the same behavior with different intentions. When I watch shows by myself, especially during the day, without doing anything else and I'm still wearing my pajamas while eating my second bowl of cereal, it's a numbing behavior (selfish). When I watch a show at the end of the day with my husband and all the kids are in bed, the house is quiet, and I'm allowing myself to decompress, it's therapeutic (self-care). It depends on the intention and the feeling afterward. If you finish an activity and afterward feel rested and recharged, that is therapeutic. If you feel no different than you did before you started, possibly worse, that is numbing.

Being able to identify these shame-deflecting behaviors takes practice and honesty. The tough skills of introspection and accountability are divine gifts. As humans, we can take a step back from our behavior and recognize a larger picture, seeing which factors of that picture are helpful and which are not. We can evaluate ourselves in a way that taps into more internal values, hopefully allowing us to recenter on what is most important. If you look at animals, you'll notice they are only capable of being in the now. In some ways, it's beautiful how animals are present in the moment. We can implement elements of that to better our experiences. Yet, an animal does not possess the ability to think "I just peed all over my owner's floor. That probably made him frustrated. Why did I pee all over? Was I scared? Was I excited? If I continue this behavior, how will it affect me and the people I love most?" No, this doesn't happen for animals. We have a remarkable opportunity to understand our lives and our behaviors and continue to evolve. Evolve in a way that allows us more meaning and less suffering.

PRACTICE

Take some time to fill out the following chart. You may or may not have answers for every box. Try to be thorough in evaluating your experiences with each of these shame deflectors. NOTE: You may also recognize shame-deflecting behaviors that don't fit into any category. These examples are not exhaustive. If that happens, please make your own additional boxes. This exercise is designed to answer one important question: ***"When I feel shame, what behaviors do I use to avoid or deflect that feeling?"***

	Blame	Judgment	Withdrawal	People Pleasing	Addictions/ Numbing	Other
Areas this shows up for me						
What/who helps						
What/who doesn't help						

CHAPTER 5

Perfectionism

I DO A LOT OF PUBLIC SPEAKING. I OFTEN SPEAK ON MENTAL HEALTH issues like anxiety and depression. Every once in a while, they let me choose the topic. This happened one summer when the women of my church asked me to speak at an annual women's retreat. Most of my speaking opportunities had been with the youth and mostly aimed at mental health awareness and coping. While I do enjoy those groups, this was the first time in a long time I was asked to speak to women about anything I wanted! I knew early on that the topic I wanted to speak on was perfectionism.

    I started out by having the women close their eyes and take several deep breaths. I wanted them to tune into their bodies for a moment and pay attention to their physical responses when I said the word "perfectionism." I started there because I knew this word was so charged and conditioned with pressures and anxieties through everyday experiences of it. Whenever I hear the word, I feel immediate pressure on my shoulders and my heart starts to race a little. If I think about it for too long, my head will start to hurt slightly. There was one woman that felt peace when she heard the word; however, as we investigated her experiences further, she realized she needed perfection to feel peace. She was definitely a self-proclaimed perfectionist. Another woman felt the urge to "leave it the hell alone." She said she didn't want to go anywhere near that, as if it were an infectious disease.

It is important to have a working definition of what I mean by perfectionism. There are many people who consider themselves perfectionists because they like things to look, feel, and operate neatly. They like order and structure. This is not exactly what I mean. Perfectionism is the persistent need to "live, look, and act" perfectly in order to avoid any perceived judgment or criticism. The effort to be perfect is focused on what other people think, as well as maintaining personal and social expectations.

In her book, *The Gifts of Imperfection*, Brené Brown finds it better to discuss what perfectionism is not as a way of understanding more clearly. She says:

> Perfectionism is not the same thing as striving to be your best. Perfectionism is not about healthy achievement and growth. Perfectionism is the belief that if we live perfect, look perfect, and act perfect, we can minimize or avoid the pain of blame, judgment, and shame. It's a shield. Perfectionism is a twenty-ton shield that we lug around thinking it will protect us when, in fact, it's the thing that's really preventing us from taking flight.
>
> Perfectionism is not self-improvement. Perfectionism is, at its core, about trying to earn approval and acceptance. Most perfectionists are praised for achievement and performance (grades, manners, rule-following, people-pleasing, appearance, sports). Somewhere along the way, we adopt this dangerous and debilitating belief system: I am what I accomplish and how well I accomplish it. Please. Perform. Perfect. Healthy striving is self-focused—How can I improve? Perfectionism is other-focused—What will they think? (Brown, *Gifts of Imperfection*).

This way of living is exhausting for two reasons. We never really can be perfect all the time and on the occasion that we actually are perfect—like first chair in orchestra, winner of the race, 100% on a test—we then have to work extra hard to maintain that perfection and reputation. This sets us up for the completely unavoidable experience of pressure, stress, and anxiety. I have worked with many perfectionists, some affectionately call themselves "recovering perfectionists," and they are highly anxious and overwhelmed all the time.

In Chapter One, I told the story of Jack and how he was able to understand vulnerability to be beautiful. Jack was also an extreme perfectionist. He came to me toward the end of the semester, and we only had a few sessions together. Still, they were powerful sessions. About ten months later, I got an email from Jack giving me a little update on his life and thanking me for our time together. I felt impressed to ask Jack if I could share his story. He was excited and told me, "I know from personal experience how uplifting it can be for people who are going through hard times to hear about people who have found a brighter path."

Per my request, he sent me an email of what he valued most from his experience in counseling. He even gave me permission to share his photo so people could better relate to an actual person. This was a magical moment for me because I believe in the power of stories. As a therapist, I am privy to amazing people and their stories, but I don't usually have the freedom to share those stories. I cherish their trust and respect the laws that bind me to confidentiality. I do wish more could be shared. When we share our true stories, we come closer to loved ones and God.

Jack was a traditional Christian. He felt a lot of pressure from the social and doctrinal expectations. Jack wrote this:

> I have had experiences in the past that taught me that my Heavenly Father loves me and my Redeemer loves me without reservation. I have felt their love, and it changed my life. I had lots of beautiful experiences, got married within the faith, and went to college. I think I expected that doing these things would fix all my problems. You know, I was doing everything I was supposed to, so I ought to feel pretty good. But I still had serious challenges. I doubted myself, I frequently felt disappointed for not being "more perfect." Not being more obedient, not reading more of the scriptures, not doing better on that talk, or making a better comment in church. And in my life outside of church, I was always beating myself up. I didn't score as high as that student. I need to go to the gym. I need to be more social. I felt that I was failing to measure up to everything

I was supposed to be. I would often compare myself to others. It wasn't so much that I believed I could *never* be as good or spiritual or whatever as the people I was comparing myself to, it was that I believed that if I could be as good as them I would finally be happy and all my problems would be solved. But the way I viewed myself, I was forever falling short.

This all kind of came to a head last winter. I was taking some really hard math and physics classes, my wife was expecting our boy, we were running out of money, and I felt this intense pressure to impress every person I had a relationship with and to measure up to what they expected me to accomplish—especially my in-laws and extended family. It got to the point where I was emotionally and physically exhausted every day. This affected how I did in school and how much I felt the Spirit, and my life started to spiral out of control. I started to believe I was doomed. I was going to fail. It was just a matter of time before it all came crashing down and everyone realized what a fraud I really was. I started to think that it would be better for my wife and our son if I wasn't there to mess everything up. So they didn't have to see me fail. I felt like being perfect and being successful in *everything* held more value than my own life. Even though, deep down, I knew that was all wrong, it was still the prevailing feeling in my heart. I didn't know what to do.

Jack was so overwhelmed with the need to please and be good enough that his anxiety, depression, and self-loathing were at top capacity. I will address more about his story later.

Anxiety is a basic worry. Something we all experience to some degree. Anxiety becomes a real problem when the person finds themselves unable to function normally and maintain responsibilities. This is often coupled with panic attacks.

The anxiety is a result of four things that feed the perfectionism:

- projection
- comparison
- self-criticism
- fear of failure

CHAPTER 5: PERFECTIONISM

Projection

Projection is when we place our emotions, fears, and judgments on those around us. We assume that everyone feels and thinks the same as we do. As a teenager, I had really bad acne. I was extremely self-conscious of it. I felt most anxious about it when I was in large crowds because I felt like everyone around me noticed my acne and how awful I looked. I assumed they judged me as harshly as I did. In reality, people probably didn't notice it at all, and if they did, they didn't change their opinion of me as a result. There are three different types of projection based on Freudian psychology: neurotic, complementary, and complimentary. My experience with acne is an example of complementary, or when we assume everyone thinks the same as us. Complimentary is similar, but we assume everyone is as skilled and capable as we are—we're particularly good at cooking, or music, or athletics and we think others can perform the same way.

As we grow into adulthood, we form and develop our own set of values that govern how we act. It is easy to assume that our set of values is the same as everyone else's. Neurotic projection works on a self-preservation level. We can project as a way to avoid our most uncomfortable emotions. This is a defense mechanism. An example of this may be a person who struggles with infidelity and is in a constant state of fear that the spouse is also cheating.

Perfectionists assume that the world demands the same level of perfection of them that they do. When they fall short of their expectations, they have this perception of great judgment and ridicule from everyone around them. However, understanding this problem and changing that perception is a huge help. The simple idea of acceptance, knowing that people are meant to act, feel, and think differently, makes a big impact on the way we see ourselves. This idea leads to the even higher principle that our different lives and experiences mean that there is no "right way" to be. We are allowed to try our best, succeed and fail, and it's all okay. I see that as a difference in the clients I work with. When I hear things like: "I feel like my friends will make fun of me, but I know they probably won't." "I worry that my husband wants me to be skinnier, but he has never said anything to lead me to assume that. It's probably all me." Or, "People probably don't notice when I say things wrong, but I still worry about it,"

I have more confidence in their overall shame resilience because they allow themselves and others to be different and have their own, often unknown, opinions.

Comparison

I addressed comparison in Chapter Three, but it is such a significant problem with perfectionists that it is worth addressing again. Perfectionists are masters at comparison. Their fuel comes from assessing their competition in order to measure up. They are perfect at certain things and the struggle then becomes trying to maintain that perfection. If they are the best (meaning better than everyone else they are comparing themselves to), they have to stay the best. I often think about this with athletes. There are some who are very driven by the pressure to stay on top. Failure is not an option. At times, this is an expectation placed on them by parents or coaches but most heavily heaped on by themselves. These athletes are stressed and depressed. However, there are other athletes that seem to be driven by something else. They have this motivation to push themselves to be their best and are not overly concerned about comparing themselves to others. Let's be clear that people can strive for greatness in an emotionally-healthy way. It is all about the intent. The difficulty lies in executing that improvement while maintaining focus on ourselves and our goals.

I often explain this by discussing the difference between being *inwardly* focused verses *outwardly* focused. Say that I want to start running and I have decided to train for my first marathon. This is something that is new and exciting for me. If I am outwardly focused, I am very occupied with comparison. I have identified the "important people," whether they are other people I run with, famous runners, or trainers I follow online. I am always very aware of how they look, what they say, and the things they post online. These are the people in the know, so I have to do, say, and look exactly like them. I have to eat what they say to eat. I have to train the way they train. If I am with them, I notice their muscles look so much better than mine. When we finish running, they are barely breathing hard while I feel like I am going to pass out.

Then comes the race. I am feeling extremely anxious. I am prepared with all the snacks, clothes, and other stuff I am "supposed" to have. I am very aware of where I start in the pack. I make note of every person that passes me and each time it feels like a punch to the gut. In distance running, people often "hit a wall." When I hit that wall, my self-criticism blows up. I have to push myself through because the worst thing in the world would be to stop or appear weak. Then, if I actually endure my onslaught of comparison and criticism and manage to finish, I will go directly to the results board so I can analyze those results with a fine-tooth comb. I want to see where I finished and who beat me, how old or young they are, and on and on. Chances are, after a race like that, I will not want to do it again unless "the people" do. Then, of course, I will have to.

If I am *inwardly* focused, my experience will be very different. While training, I may look at training plans, but I try to find something that makes me feel comfortable, confident, and fits into my schedule. I may pick a plan and adjust it a little to make it right for me. As I am training, I am trying to push myself a little more all the time. I may still be learning things and watching or talking to other people. As I do, I still try to find my fit in the suggestions they give or ideas they present. During my training, I find this surprising sense of accomplishment as I go farther and possibly faster than I ever expected. I don't get too preoccupied with regard to what other people are doing. I try to focus on my own experience.

Then comes the race. I have prepared in a way that helps me feel calm and not anxious. I wear my most comfortable clothes and have my favorite energy snacks. I have a music playlist that I enjoy and have found my own way to fuel and hydrate for the race. As I run, I am trying to focus on my breath and pace. I let myself enjoy the experience. I look around and find joy in my surroundings. People may be passing me, but I'm also passing others. I may come to "hit that wall." Making this a positive experience is my goal, so I slow down or stop. I try to take my time to stretch or walk a little until I am ready to run again. When I finish, I feel good. This was a whole new experience. I learned so much about myself and how I could push myself more than

I expected. That satisfaction was all I needed. My chances of repeating this race experience are very likely.

Can you see how the way we motivate ourselves to improve and the level at which we compare ourselves can make a huge difference in our performance? Interestingly enough, these two versions of the race may look exactly the same from the outside. I may have finished at the same time and done all the same things. However, the internal experience was vastly different. When we are supportive and encourage ourselves, especially when we fall, we have higher chances for success.

Self-Criticism

When it comes to perfectionism, we cannot leave self-criticism out. Perfectionists are masters at finding and dwelling on the imperfect, so it is natural to be critical. That "eye for the flaw" creates a perpetual burden. To the rest of us, a perfectionist may look and seem perfect. Inside their own head, they are constantly identifying what needs to be better and shaming themselves because of it. Again, in *The Gifts of Imperfection*, Brown says that shame is the birthplace of perfectionism. To perfectionists, their mind is the worst bully of all. This feeds back to the anxiety which becomes a physical, emotional, and mental battle.

Going back to Jack's story, he demonstrated all of these classic behaviors. He felt others held the same unreasonably high expectations for him as he did. He constantly compared himself to those he felt to be superior. His self-criticism was so suffocating that he became suicidal. During our first several sessions, Jack was learning and thinking as he tried to internalize the ideas, but everything came to a big turning point for him. It happened when we did the "empty chair" exercise. He said:

> The thing that finally changed this was when you pulled a chair in front of me and told me to pretend six-year-old me was sitting in it. You told me to talk to him and tell him everything I would have wanted him to hear at that age. I think you chose six as the age

because I said that was the last time I remembered feeling confident or proud of who I was. It was really awkward at first. But once I started talking, the words just came spilling out and I started to cry. I remembered everything that happened in my life at that age and all of the things I felt at that time. I knew that six-year-old boy deserved love and mercy because "he is awesome," and I just wanted him to know that. Then I realized that boy is still me, I am still the same, and I still deserve the same thing. It completely changed the way I treat myself. After I left your office, I decided, and I was able to really believe, I deserve this. I decided to accept myself and treat myself with respect. To treat me how I wished six-year-old me had been treated.

It wasn't too late to help him, because I *am* him! It was such a freeing realization. I am a child of God! I matter to Him! So He loves it when I honor and respect myself! It hurts Him when I do not, because He sees me the way I saw six-year-old me. As a child who deserves nothing but love and acceptance. How could I turn my back on Jesus Christ by treating myself as anything less than a very special person that He loves and died for? I decided to be honest and try my hardest, and then be satisfied, regardless of the results, and regardless of what others may perceive about me. My mental health is more important than what others think of me, no matter how much I value their opinion. I have been so much happier. I don't think about ending my life anymore. I don't beat myself up over stupid things. I am comfortable with who I am.

Now, with all this talk about perfectionists, it may be easy to say, "That's not me. I know I am imperfect and I'm okay with that." Such may be the truth for many of you. I want to examine this a little further because being a perfectionist may not be the same as struggling with perfectionism, even though the behaviors are the same.

I want you to evaluate your self-talk. What are the areas where you are most critical and harsh about yourself? What are the areas where "failure" is unacceptable? Then, what are the areas where you are okay with being less than perfect? When you mess up, are you able to let it go? Use the following table to write down your responses.

Areas where I am nice to myself What do I say? Where can I "fail" safely?	Areas where I am NOT nice to myself. What do I say? Where am I most harsh and critical?

My Example

Areas where I am nice to myself What do I say? Where can I "fail" safely?	Areas where I am NOT nice to myself. What do I say? Where am I most harsh and critical?
—When I'm around my kids and family —As a wife —When I'm exercising by myself —With my body around strangers —Appearing goofy	—When I'm around colleagues —When I'm exercising around other people —As a parent —With my body around people I know and respect —My ability to stay on top of things

I am a big advocate of embracing our imperfections and sharing our "failures." In fact, I often intentionally put the word failure in quotations because that word is never defined the same from one person to the next. We make up our own definitions for failure. I would not say that I am a perfectionist; however, I do struggle with perfectionism. I am good at letting go if I embarrass myself in public. That is in my "nice to myself" column. I can look goofy and say words wrong and it doesn't turn into self-criticism. I am also okay with not knowing all the answers. Even as a therapist I say, "I don't know" all the time. These are not failures to me.

However, my critical self shows up in large doses when I can't stay on top of all my responsibilities. I feel like a big failure when my house is trashed (which is all the time because I invited tiny humans to live with me). I feel pressure as a mother and as a homemaker to look perfect to all the other mothers—which is ironic because, at my core, being a good homemaker isn't very important to me. But when people come to my house and my floor is dirty and smudgy, my inner critic says, "Erika, they are going to judge you and think you are a dirty mess."

When I have a breakdown in the middle of the bedtime routine, I think, "Erika, you can't handle any of this. You are not a good mother. Other mothers do this every night with twice as many kids, and they can hold it together. Then they go make homemade bread afterward!" (That bread part is a joke against myself because I have never made homemade bread and grew up with a mother who made it all the time.)

When I am struggling with a client and they just don't seem to be making progress, I think, "They obviously should be working with someone more competent. You aren't very good at this therapy stuff. You just like the idea of helping people, but you probably aren't." So I compare. I project how I feel about myself onto those around me. I let my critical voice have at it. I am not a perfectionist, but I still struggle with the pressure to be perfect.

Fear of Failure

I know firsthand that for women, the pressure to measure up is real, which is unfortunate. As a society, we are making big changes to value women more. In many ways, we prize and value womanhood. "I am woman, hear me roar" kind of stuff. The best way to connect and bond as humans is to love and accept the real and honest versions of each other. Yet, we put on facades and post pictures of our perfect-looking lives and make sure that no one really knows what is going on. We do that because of the fear of looking like a failure. This is the fuel behind it all. This is why Brown calls it the 20-ton shield. It is a protection to avoid failing.

Men struggle with perfectionism, too. Sometimes I feel like they have it worse. Men feel the pressure of being "strong" enough, which does not allow room for any vulnerability. It is more socially acceptable for women to be vulnerable. Men do not always have that luxury. They may have feelings and be struggling in similar ways but to talk about it is "weak." In their roles within the home or workplace, there is often little room for them to be human. Within traditional family systems, the man has to "provide and protect." At work, it is a rat race to be promoted and make enough money and display a status of success to the world in order to achieve acceptance. That pressure is doubly hard for men that are gay or transgender or any other life expression that challenges the norm of how a "man" should live.

This is an unfortunate side effect of many conservative or religious cultures. A man's fear of failure is often reinforced by the expressed disappointment of parents, avoidance of peers, and distancing of spouses. Even when those things aren't happening, there is a lot of silence and a lack of safe places to talk. Of all the things I wish I could change, this would be one of the first. We need to talk more openly and honestly about our many failures.

There is great research on the benefits, and even the necessity, of failure in order to grow and progress. Some of the best organizations in the nation have set up a failure reward system where they celebrate when people fail and even award prizes. They believe that failure is a necessary part of the process and must happen in order to achieve success.

We hear quotes all the time that tell us that failure is good:

"Fail early, fail often, but always fail forward." —*John C. Maxwell*

"I have not failed, I have just found 10,000 ways that won't work." —*Thomas Edison*

"There is no failure, just learning experiences." —*Anonymous*

"Consider failure as a tutor, not a tragedy." —*Lynn G. Robbins*

"Success is stumbling from failure to failure without loss of enthusiasm." —*Winston Churchill*

CHAPTER 5: PERFECTIONISM

"Our destiny is not determined by the number of times we stumble but by the number of times we rise, dust ourselves off, and move forward." —*Dieter F. Uchtdorf*

I see a lot of perfectionism that focuses on spirituality and faith. Many of us have a faulty understanding of what God expects of us. I have had many conversations with people who know they don't have to be perfect for God, but deep down they *believe* they should. Even Jack said in his letter:

> I *knew* that I had eternal worth, that I had a divine destiny, and I knew the plan of salvation front to back, but there was a huge piece missing between what I knew and what I felt. My head knew I was not worthless and that I should be proud of myself, but my heart still believed I was worthless and did not deserve to be loved. My heart was telling me I was a hypocrite and a failure. I felt like I had enough evidence to justify this. I believed that everyone, even the worst people, deserved mercy and love. I just couldn't figure out how to believe I deserved it, too. I wasn't being honest enough or vulnerable enough to admit to myself that I deserved the kind of treatment I thought everyone else did.

Someone once said that the longest distance we can travel is from our head to our heart, meaning that we often understand things in our head. We get the concepts and explanations, *but* we do not really *believe* them in our heart. I find this at times within churches. People can get caught up in the expectations of being religious and feel pressured to do such things perfectly. Somewhere down the line, they begin to believe that their perfect diligence is what God expects.

This is why shame is so dangerous. It takes a person, a person well capable of higher-order thinking and awareness, and causes them to believe they are the one exception to the rule. Of course, when we are triggered emotionally, all sorts of irrational thoughts show up. Yet when we can take ourselves back to an objective place, we can ask ourselves this, "If I truly believe in the worth of all other humans, if I find true value in others, can I not understand that I am a human who deserves the same?"

My husband and I met at a rock climbing gym in college. Climbing has always been something that we enjoy doing together and with our children. Climbing is the perfect match of challenge and excitement for me. I love everything about it. The feel of the rock, the strain of my muscles, the partnership with another climber, and being outside in beautiful, high-up places. When I climb, I try to improve my climbing. I want to climb a route faster, cleaner, or even move up to a harder climb. Part of my experience of climbing is falling. Any good climber, when they are pushing for improvement and trying something hard, will literally fall—often. They will try and fall and try and fall until they succeed, but they are safely caught each time they fall. Each climber is secured to another climber on the ground by a rope. That rope and the climbing partner will always catch the climber and keep her safe.

Arguably the best big wall climber to ever live is Tommy Caldwell. He and his partner, Kevin Jorgeson, completed the first ascent of the hardest big wall climb in the world on El Capitan in Yosemite National Park. This climb was on a section of El Capitan called the Dawn Wall. That section was considered unclimbable. For years, Tommy spent time on the rock trying to find a possible route. Climbing, repelling down from the top, swinging to all areas of the rock face looking for ways to complete a climb from bottom to top. When Tommy finally decided on a route, he and Kevin started making plans to climb it. This 3,000-foot wall was broken up into small sections called pitches. To claim they climbed the entire wall, they would take turns on each pitch, climbing with the rope secured to the rock at a set point. But the climber is always climbing above the rope (Lowell & Mortimer, *The Dawn Wall*).

This is called a free-climb ascent because the climber climbs each part of the rock by himself. If he falls, the rope will catch him, but because he climbs above the set anchor point, he could fall anywhere from two to fifteen feet until the rope catches his weight. If he falls during a pitch, he has to go back to the bottom of the pitch and start over. These two men spent more than two weeks living on the rock and climbing each pitch until they finally free-climbed each section and finished triumphantly at the top. During those two weeks, they fell over and over and had to restart different pitches multiple times.

CHAPTER 5: PERFECTIONISM

At one point, Kevin could not complete one of the hardest pitches for days. He kept climbing and falling and starting over and climbing and falling and starting over again, all day long for six days! Falling was part of the process of success. They had to learn how to fall over and over and keep trying.

I imagine there was something that pushed Kevin forward and kept him from allowing doubt and despair to take over. That was hope. Whether it was a spiritual hope or not, hope allows us to put trust in something good. The goodness of succeeding, goodness in self, goodness in an experience or process. Hope is what can get us through the fall and give us the strength to get back on the rock. When our faith in ourselves is shaken, we can keep perfect or imperfect hope in the goodness of life, or God, or light, or anything that grounds us to deep meaning. Cultivate hope in something that helps you feel connected to meaning and power.

Practice

- Are you a perfectionist? If so, how?

- If you aren't a perfectionist, where do you struggle with perfectionism?

- Did your "self-critic" start in someone else's voice and then become your own? If so, whose voice?

- What experiences have you had that contribute to those critical thoughts?

- What is your relationship with failure? Just as if failure were a person you know, describe the relationship and interactions.

CHAPTER 6

Self-Awareness

As children grow up, they reach a stage after about a year or eighteen months when they are stuck between wanting to communicate and not having mastered language skills. Because of that gap between desire and ability, attempts at communication often result in a frustrated meltdown. The ability to express is cathartic and therapeutic. That experience doesn't completely change as we get older. We can have "meltdowns" of our own when we have confusing feelings inside, and we don't understand them or know how to talk about them.

Just as kids can learn how to better regulate their emotions as they learn to talk and communicate, adults can learn how to understand their emotions and what to do about them. We can feel more in control of confusing emotions when we better understand what those emotions are and why we feel them. They become emotions with names and histories, and we can work with them better.

One of my favorite moments in session is when a client has an "ah-ha" moment—a moment of clarity when something all of the sudden makes sense and comes together. When this happens, there is a shift in understanding. There is also a shift in the struggle. The perspective is less foggy, less unknown, and less difficult. The only thing that changes is awareness. In those moments, great growth happens. It can be a catalyst for more growth, more awareness, and more hope.

Brené Brown performs qualitative research, focused on understanding reasons and motives. This is different from quantitative research which utilizes numbers and data analyses to find conclusions. Her research is based on hundreds of interviews with many different kinds of people. She interviews, collects data, looks for patterns, and analyzes the results. Something interesting she found is that most people have very little vocabulary to describe their emotions. So little, in fact, that Brown's team determined these three descriptors to be the most common. Often they were the only emotions that people could identify. The emotions are happy, sad, and "pissed off." The problem with this is our emotions are far more diverse. When we can identify and describe more accurately how we feel, we are more likely to grow, connect, and understand.

I have often been around people who don't consider themselves "touchy-feely people." Now, I understand what they are saying. I still disagree. Nearly all humans are "touchy-feely." We can't help it. Whether experience with emotional expression and awareness exists or not, the feelings are always there. Some people say that they are logical in all things and don't get caught up in emotions. I think that's funny because those people may operate from a logical point, but they do that because they feel peace and truth about those logical ideas and decisions. They feel that way of thought and action to be "right." That feels balanced and settled to them. That peace is an emotion.

This is especially true for those who profess to be spiritual or have any relationship with God or a higher power. That entire experience is based on feeling. Any sense of connection outside oneself is felt. We can't get away from being creatures of emotion. Embracing that reality is productive and, for some, highly healing. At the same time, some people don't know where to begin that process.

Learning about emotions and gaining a better vocabulary is a good start to self-awareness. This is something I did a lot when I was working with young children. When I asked them about feelings and experiences that caused emotions, they needed help knowing what they felt. They had feelings but didn't always have the words to describe them. I would use an emotion chart like the free printable one at www.therapistaid.com/worksheets/printable-emotion-faces.pdf to give them ideas as well as pictures to match how they felt.

I use this same method with adults. I was raised in a community that had a lot of agricultural influence. There are many great values taught and encouraged within that lifestyle, like hard work and perseverance. However, there are other values that are not encouraged. Talking about or showing emotion is often seen as weak. The "cowboy up" or "suck it up" mentality is common. When people are raised in families and communities like this, they get very little practice identifying how they feel. They are more likely to ignore and suppress it. That also creates a small emotional vocabulary, so I understand when people come to me and really cannot put words to their feelings. They may even be invested in the therapy process and want to feel better, but they just don't know what they are feeling.

Emotions are confusing. A big part of that is because emotions have layers. You may be feeling an emotion like anger and acting angry and mean, but under that anger, you are really hurt and sad. We can easily get caught up in the distraction of superficial emotion and not pay attention to the underlying, more accurate ones. The superficial emotion is our way of coping and possibly avoiding, feeling the deeper, more painful ones.

Brené Brown shares a story about how she has tried to teach her children this and uses a simple method to help them dig deeper. She simply asks how they are feeling, and then, after talking to them for a while about that and validating them, she asks, "What is under that feeling?" Of course, her family has had a lot of practice with self-awareness and as a result, her kids have, over time, been able to understand lots of different kinds of emotions.

When my kids were smaller, one of the easiest emotions I felt was impatience. It would come out as quickly as a worm in the rain. When I got impatient, I would also start to blame. My kids weren't listening, my husband wasn't helping enough, and my dog was always getting in the way! This often happened on Sunday mornings. Ugh! Ironically, Sunday was one of the most difficult days of the week, and yet it was really important to me. It was supposed to be a day to feel close to God and feel peace. Those days often had more contention and stress than peace.

Here's how it used to go: I'd get up and get myself ready first because I had learned, the hard way, that if I didn't ready myself first, I would put all my time into getting everyone else ready and run out of time for me. Honestly, Sunday was the only day I really tried to make myself look presentable. So I was up and I was ready. If I didn't happen to have any additional early church meetings (because I was highly involved and had many different responsibilities at the time), I would start in on the kids. Between me and my three girls, I had four heads of hair to complete. For that reason, I kept my son's hair short. His head was his responsibility. Two of the three girls hated brushing their hair and it always became a fight and scream fest. One of the screamers hated it so much that I also kept her hair as short as possible. That way I wouldn't have to do much more than brush it a little and give it some curl. Even that was a struggle. While I was frantically trying to get the girls dressed in tights and find their shoes and argue about what dress to wear, I'd nag at my son to get dressed and do his hair.

Of course, we had to fit in lunch or breakfast for everyone before we left. My husband usually worked on that and helped nag my son. While all of that was happening, our kitchen got trashed. That also stressed me out because I knew I'd have to come home and clean up all that mess just to turn around and mess it up again to make dinner. I wanted my husband to clean, too, but didn't ask him. I just expected him to do it. Because he hadn't mastered the art of reading my mind, that made me even more frustrated.

One kid would freak out about her shoes "feeling funny," and the other kids would start fighting with each other. I'd have a couple of minutes to get in the car and I wouldn't even have my shoes on. If I had to teach a lesson that day, I usually hadn't even started to prepare. I'd have to read and prepare during the first part of church which is nearly impossible because I'd be sitting with my four kids that were driving me crazy! By the time I got in the car, I'd already lost my cool four times (meaning that I didn't just yell, I'd ogre yell, like Shrek does when his swamp is being taken over by fantasy creatures). Five of the six of us would finally be in the car and I'd be near tears as I wailed on the horn. I'd have nothing left and knew I hadn't even gotten to church yet.

Let's break this down. The top-level or superficial emotion is impatience. That is pretty transparent and you can see that frustration

CHAPTER 6: SELF-AWARENESS

is underneath. Under the frustration is a lot more stuff. For one, it is Sunday. I try to make my family look nice—not only are we supposed to look our best (which should be the only motivation for me to make them look nice), but I feel the pressure to make them look better than nice. They have to look close to perfect. No stains on their clothes, no flyaways or frizz, and no food in their hair (very difficult objectives some days). My son has to have clothes that match and a "less wrinkled" shirt (I gave up on ironing a while ago). I have to look good because all those other ladies are so stylish and I feel pressure. Under the frustration is pressure to look good, coming from the shame that tells me "we don't look good enough." And to avoid all this uncomfortable ugly emotion, I blame and yell and cry. Here are the emotions:

Impatience with getting ready
Frustration with how much I have to do
Pressure to look good
Shame that my family and I don't look good enough

Here are some more emotions that boiled up as well:

Impatience with my kids' bickering
Frustration with how irrational they are being
Anger that my kids are fighting so much and not listening to me
Shame that I am not a good enough mother to teach them how to get along better

Impatience that there is not enough time to do everything
Anxiety that I have to finish my lesson
Fear that I won't get it done and will have to "wing it"
Shame that I am not a good teacher and can't prepare or teach at all

All of these emotions seemed to be covering up shame. That's not always the case and it may not even go down four levels of emotion. However, the better a person is at self-awareness, the more layers there can be. In my experience, shame is the root more often than not. Also, something to note is that with this personal example, the entire experience was triggering. My prefrontal cortex was less than functional.

That made me more irrational, anxious, and stressed as well as less understanding that everyone else in my family was probably struggling as well. It wasn't all about *me*. It's rarely all about us.

In order to deal well with our shame, we must first see it. I tell clients, "Watch your shame. See where it lives, what it looks like, who it hangs out with and who it doesn't." We may be triggered by situations and not really see it as shame unless we look closely. Our shame can be triggered and send us into an emotional spin. As a way to avoid shame, we engage in poor behaviors. When we understand what triggers those emotions, we are either quicker to act and prevent the bad behaviors, or we avoid the trigger altogether. My triggers are looking and acting perfectly like mothers in the church and cheerleaders as well as Sunday mornings in general. We can't always avoid triggers but at least we can be ready for them, like when you are in the ocean and try to remain standing when a wave hits. You brace for it.

Once you know more about the nature of your shame, you can give it a name or put words to it. What is the shame telling me? The most important reason we need to do that is so we can create distance and space between us and the lies that shame tells us. We immediately think, "I am not attractive enough," when we need to see it as, "My shame is making me feel not attractive enough." That is more of a feeling than an identity. For any emotion, it is healthier to make that separation. "I am a person that experiences depression or anxiety," not "I am a depressed person." That small shift makes a difference over time. At first, it may be semantics and a change in the words we use, but emotionally, it gives permission to be who we are and not what we experience.

Nietzsche says, "To live is to suffer, to survive is to find meaning in the suffering." Emotions can be difficult and painful. The process of understanding those emotions can be even more difficult and painful. If, in the end, we find understanding, meaning, and purpose, then it is for our good. This is like the process of muscle growth. When a person exercises and pushes their muscles, the small mini fibers in the muscles actually tear apart. Then the immune system steps in to repair the muscles and make them bigger and better prepared for exercise. The process of tearing and repairing the muscles are repeated over and over to make them stronger. Emotional awareness may feel painful, but it is the pathway to redemption, healing, and growth.

PRACTICE

This is a multi-day self-awareness exercise that can help broaden your understanding of your experiences. Journaling is a simple tool that has been proven to be very effective in helping people understand their emotions better and feel better about them. I would suggest using a journal for these exercises.

- For five days, set a timer to go off every two hours during the daytime hours. Every time the alarm goes off, write down, "I feel _____." And you cannot use the words happy, sad, or mad.

- For an additional five days, change the timer to go off every four hours. Answer the same question but add, "and that causes my body to feel ____(sensation)____ in/on/around _____(location)_____."

- For the last five days, keep the timer at every four hours. This time write, "I feel _____. The emotions under that feeling are _____."

CHAPTER 7

Vulnerability, Empathy, and Boundaries

VULNERABILITY

IF CONNECTION IS THE PATH THAT LEADS TO JOY AND FULFILLMENT, then vulnerability is the machine that paves the path. Sincere connection does not happen without vulnerability. Vulnerability is especially important to me because that is where my journey with all this research and writing started. When I saw Brené Brown's first TED Talk, it changed so much for me. I remember I was cooking in my kitchen watching the video with my husband. Her ideas seemed to be perfectly in line with my personal core values. At that point in my life, I felt a near tangible craving for more authenticity and connection with people. Up until then, I had been feeling very jaded socially.

Hearing Brown speak was invigorating, like jumping into cold lake water where all my faculties became alert and focused. It was more than just the research and findings. It was her. She presented in such a way that included herself. She, an accomplished professor, researcher, speaker, and writer, stood on the stage. She not only talked about vulnerability, but she also demonstrated it. She explained how her research stimulated a mid-life crisis for her and through more work, therapy, and learning, she was able to move through it.

That video sold me on the idea that being authentic is a necessary part of joy. Authenticity feels vulnerable at times. She says, "Vulnerability is the birthplace of love, belonging, joy, courage, empathy, and creativity. It is the source of hope, empathy, accountability, and authenticity. If we want greater clarity in our purpose or deeper and more meaningful spiritual lives, vulnerability is the path." (Brown, *Daring Greatly,* 2015).

From that point on, I ate up everything she said and wrote like it was the newest drug on the market. It spoke to my soul and motivated my heart. I wanted to be my most honest self in everything I did.

Thinking about vulnerability makes me smile for two reasons. It was my start, and because I'm able to smile about vulnerability. That seems ironic. Vulnerability is not an experience that makes us, as a society, smile much. It is uncomfortable, anxiety-ridden, and scary. That is why many people categorize vulnerability as bad, weak, and unnecessary. Part of that is from how the word is defined; "the quality or state of being exposed to the possibility of being attacked or harmed, either physically or emotionally." It also means, "willingness to show emotion or to allow one's weakness to be seen or known; willingness to risk being hurt or attacked." (Brown, *Daring Greatly*, 2015).

On an emotional level, vulnerability has different meanings for different people. I wrongly assumed that vulnerability was just about talking openly and honestly. Indeed it is that, but it's also many other things. It can be trying to make new friends, starting a new job, asking a professor for help, telling someone you love them, or even doing push-ups in the gym. As a professional, I feel very vulnerable when I don't have all the answers and I can't help people as much as I think I should.

I define vulnerability as any time we are trying to be, do, or say something that is honest about who we are. We feel exposed and fear the risk of negative consequences (like judgment). That's why vulnerability is different for different people. Many people like doing push-ups because they are good at it and find satisfaction in pushing themselves (not to mention the added attention they may get for doing so). Doing push-ups in the gym makes me very self-conscious. I worry, "Am I doing it right? Are people noticing how bad my form is? Surely they saw that I only did three." But if I do those push-ups anyway and struggle through the anxiety and self-criticism, I am doing them because I want to get stronger. If I can hold to that center of self, I will do it anyway, despite the vulnerable discomfort.

CHAPTER 7: VULNERABILITY, EMPATHY, AND BOUNDARIES

At a certain point, we come to a decision—either we choose to be vulnerable, which means caring more about staying true to ourselves than about the fear of what others may think, or we don't and we continue to hide or limit ourselves. The biggest irony of all is that most people value seeing vulnerability in others. We see it as brave. When I see people do something I deem vulnerable, like admitting to a client that they don't know everything, I am inspired. I had a pediatrician who was really good at that. As the mother of his patient, I saw he was very honest, and it built my trust in him. I knew that if he didn't know something, he would be honest and then work to find more information. Also, when he *did* know the answers, I could trust that information because he told me when he didn't have the answers.

Think of someone you've seen lately doing something brave and ask yourself if that was also vulnerable. In order to practice vulnerability, we have to challenge the idea that it can be brave for other people but weak for ourselves.

Brené Brown shares an analogy about this comparing being vulnerable to being in a battle arena. If we are trying often enough to be brave, we will most definitely be punched and thrown to the ground. It was this part that I failed to understand for quite some time. I just saw being vulnerable as being real and there was no way that could go wrong. Over time, after some wounds and bruises of my own, I understood things better.

For me, church provided many opportunities to be vulnerable. There was one time in Sunday school we were discussing some chapters in the New Testament. I don't remember the exact place, but it was one of Paul's epistles. The teacher asked us to look through the chapters and talk about the areas we liked. As I read, there was a section I definitely *did not* like. It was one of several places where Paul was talking about women and marriage and using words like "submit." It reminded me of an experience I had with a woman who attended church with my parents and spoke about these epistles. She had said something like, "I really love and appreciate and enjoy studying these chapters. I have come to the conclusion that I am not a big fan of Paul, but that's okay. I still find deep meaning in my study." When I heard that from her, I thought, "Wow, we can say that out loud? Because that is how I feel! Paul isn't my favorite either!" It was important for me to hear that and give myself permission to like or not like things I studied.

As I sat in that Sunday school class, I felt impressed to share my thoughts. "I actually didn't like chapter three because…." This comment was made right after a man from my church (a man of very high standing and leadership) had just commented on all the good things he liked about that same chapter. Probably not the best timing, but I had to say something. I was trying to show up and be seen because I knew I wasn't the only person who felt that way. I was the only one willing to say it out loud.

After my comment, there were lots of responses. Some people explained their perspectives. A few agreed. More were concerned about my "heathenish ideas." They wanted to help me "see the truth." At least, that's how it seemed. I didn't feel validated, at all. After class, it continued. That man, who was a leader, stood in line to talk to me. There was literally a line. He wanted to help me understand those scriptures better, or correctly. I didn't hold it against those people because I knew they were speaking their truth. I respected that very much. I just didn't hold the same truth. I didn't agree and that was okay. I wasn't damned because of it. I was just being honest.

I was definitely judged that day by others. People probably had all sorts of concerns about my spirituality and salvation. However, it was more important for me to be vulnerable and speak honestly than to just sit and listen. It was important to be my true self, no matter what.

People ask, "Why be vulnerable when it is hard and sometimes it beats you down?" That takes us back to the beginning; vulnerability is the pathway to connection. Even if that connection is solely experienced within yourself. Even when being vulnerable beats us up, it will reward us with more belonging and self-love. We just have to keep at it. And it's always worth it. For me, in that Sunday school class, the majority of people didn't empathize or understand me. They were trying to change my opinion and my emotions. However, there was a small number who did understand. Some of them talked to me afterward. That helped me feel better about myself and more connected to them. I felt safe to be myself with those people. Even if no one had understood me, it still would have been worth it—for me to be open,

CHAPTER 7: VULNERABILITY, EMPATHY, AND BOUNDARIES

vulnerable, and true to myself. After coming through that, I felt more in touch with myself. Self-honesty is worth the risk of judgment.

Another example was when I was working with a female client and we were discussing a certain relationship she had with a friend. They were really close and spent almost every day together. She was starting to develop feelings for him and wasn't sure if he felt the same way. Sometimes in sessions, I like to play out the "worst case scenario" to see how it feels. I said, "How would you feel if you told him about your feelings and he respectfully told you he didn't feel the same way?" She mimicked a dying sound and said, "Ugh! That would be terrible. I would feel rotten and embarrassed!"

Several sessions later, because she was a very brave person that really valued being authentic, she told me she did talk to him about her feelings. She put all her cards on the table. He respectfully told her he didn't feel the same way. It was exactly the worst-case scenario we had imagined. However, as I talked to her about this experience, being honest with her friend brought out many things in their relationship that she didn't see before. Although she still felt terrible and embarrassed, she did *not* regret it. It felt good to be honest and open even though he didn't have the reaction she had hoped for. I thought that was very impressive. I fully expected her to say, "I will never be vulnerable again." Instead, she became more invested in living true to herself.

Did Christ also feel vulnerable at times? I don't have an answer for that. I'm not sure Christ felt fear and discomfort the same way we do, but it is a fascinating idea to think about.

The main purpose of practicing honest vulnerabilities is because it leads to true connections. People can connect over all sorts of things: interests, jobs, similarities in family or background, talents, and hobbies. Sincere emotional connection happens on a deeper level. Because of the courage it takes to be vulnerable, when you come through it with a person who loves you anyway, or loves you more, there is a unique bonding experience that takes place. This is similar to the Florence Nightingale effect, in which a patient falls in love with their nurse, or vice versa. The original meaning of this effect refers to the empathetic connection a caretaker/rescuer and patient/victim can feel for one another.

Say, for example, I was in a car accident. I was alone in the car and crashed into a tree off the side of the road. Maybe I crashed because I was texting and wasn't paying attention. I was alone and hurt for a long time, feeling a lot of fear and pain. I also felt a whole heap of shame because I was texting and driving, and that's a stupid thing to do. Then comes a paramedic who sees me all beaten up and bruised. He cares for me. He helps me feel safe and hopeful. There is no judgment by this paramedic. He doesn't care about the texting and doesn't think I'm stupid. He just cares for me. I feel very vulnerable in those initial moments and fear that others will see. When I push through that fear and find out someone still cares about me, I feel closer to him. I feel bonded. Even if I never see that paramedic again, I will have a feeling of connection to him, always. Scientifically, similar things are happening in my brain that cause me to feel connected to the paramedic. It's similar to how I feel connected to my sister when I have a vulnerable conversation with her. It is that connection that makes us feel alive and fulfilled, with a sense of purpose. Connection is a major pathway to joy.

Empathy

In her second TED Talk, Brené Brown explains that empathy is the antidote to shame. She says that "If you put shame in a petri dish, it needs three things to grow exponentially: secrecy, silence, and judgment. If you put the same amount of shame in a petri dish and douse it with empathy, it can't survive" (Brown, *Gifts of Imperfection*). A major requirement for empathy is to be able to experience your own feelings as well as the other person's feelings. For some, that can be too much, especially when their own emotions are too difficult to tolerate alone. I have heard people describe themselves as "over feelers" or "empaths." As they continue to explain, they tell me they feel other people's feelings so much that they take on those emotions. That makes it hard to hear another person's struggle or provide support adequately. These people think that is empathy. Because they cannot maintain their own emotions as well as the other person's, it is something else. Yes, feeling empathy causes emotions and, at times, can

CHAPTER 7: VULNERABILITY, EMPATHY, AND BOUNDARIES

make us feel various negative things. However, if those things become unbearable, you have lost the empathetic connection.

I see it like swimming lessons. Say I am a swim instructor and I am trying to swim in the deep end with my student. She is scared and wary. She has never swam in the deep end before. It helps that I'm there. At first, I have to hold onto them in the water. I have to be strong enough as a swimmer to support my weight in the water and some of theirs. If I cannot do that, my support as a swim instructor is void. She cannot rely on me in any way if I am struggling and halfway drowning. Emotionally, we have to be able to support our own feelings and experiences as well as someone else's. It takes self-awareness work to determine if we can maintain that balance. For certain circumstances, the "swim student" is too large to support, or their struggle is too large. If I am a rape survivor and the experience is still recent, I may not be able to be empathetic with another survivor because their words trigger my own emotions. It's too "heavy" to hold.

Personally, I am less competent in my empathy with my kids. It is really hard to practice empathy when we are triggered. I am great at empathy in my work, but sometimes with my kids, I get triggered. I can't support my emotions *and* theirs at the same time. My kid is throwing a fit because she hates the way her pants feel and I cannot handle my feelings of frustration and shame because I think I should have taught her more self-control (as if that is a thing you can really teach). So, I get preoccupied with my emotions, not allowing me to stop and recognize that she literally cannot tolerate the sensation of light touch with clothing and has a sensory disorder that causes her to freak out. The sensation is overwhelming for her. If I was able to manage my stress response better, I could recognize how tough it is when I lose control of myself (again, my ogre yelling). It's so hard when I know I should be acting differently but my emotions get so intense that I cannot keep them still. Her fits trigger my frustration so I cannot tread water for the both of us. Times like that are hard for both parties. One wants to be empathetic and supportive but can't, and the other needs empathy to heal and doesn't get it.

For people like me who want to be better "swim instructors," it takes practice and a lot of self-awareness. When my daughter throws a fit, my emotional reaction happens almost instantly, which means that my prefrontal cortex shuts off. If I breathe, slow down, and recognize what is going on for me, I am better able to tolerate my feelings, balance out my nervous system, and be patient and empathetic toward her. However, if you are my daughter and a swimmer with a failing "swim instructor," it's important to accept that the instructor can't swim well enough to support you yet. That is a very hard truth to accept, especially when it is with important people in our lives. Some parents and spouses and friends are not always able to be empathetic with their kids, and it's important to find other people to give them that.

Another important part of empathy is to understand that it is *not* advice. Advice usually comes when you are practicing sympathy. Sympathy wants to "fix" the problem from a safe, emotional distance. Unless someone is directly asking for advice or opinions, don't give them. Many times, when a person is struggling emotionally, they know exactly what to do that would help. However, either they can't do it yet or they need time to allow the feelings to run their course. "I failed a math test, and now I have to retake it. I know that in order to do better I have to study a different way, but I just feel so bad about that F. I can't help but feel like a failure. I need someone to sit with me in that sucky feeling of failure and avoid telling me all the best ways to study and prepare to retake the test." Or, "I looked at pornography again. I need someone to help me with the shame and let me know I still have worth, not give a long discourse on how bad pornography is and how it will ruin my life." Or, "I feel ugly and unattractive. When others tell me I'm pretty and looks don't matter, it doesn't help. It especially doesn't help when they give me beauty or fitness tips. It's like they don't understand how much shame I feel about my body."

My favorite example of the healing power of empathy is explained in the shortest verse in all the scriptures. Christ was very close to two sisters and their brother (Mary, Martha, and Lazarus). They were his dear friends. The siblings lived in Bethany and Lazarus became sick. Christ heard about the illness and was busy preaching far away. He stayed two days and then told his disciples that he needed to go to Bethany. On his journey back, he was given the impression that Lazarus had died. When he was approaching the house, Martha ran out to him to greet him. She broke down immediately when she saw

CHAPTER 7: VULNERABILITY, EMPATHY, AND BOUNDARIES

him, sobbing as he hugged her. He tried to tell her that it would be okay and that her "brother shall rise again." Martha thought he was referring to the resurrection and didn't know how literal Christ was being. They both went into the house where Mary met them with the same response as her sister. At this point, Christ's empathy increased. "He groaned in the spirit, and was troubled."

Of course, all along he loved these sisters and didn't want them to experience such sorrow. But his love evolved into empathy as he hugged them both, feeling their sadness. He knew such sorrow because he also loved Lazarus, even though he knew he was capable of bringing him back. At that moment, he didn't assure them and tell them what he planned to do. No, instead, "Jesus wept." He wept *with* them. He connected with these women and felt right along with them. The story continues, and Christ is taken to the tomb where he raises Lazarus from the dead. This was the first time Christ had performed such a miracle. As amazing as that was, I believe that the moments of connection and empathy were just as powerful. When Mary and Martha cried *with* Christ, they felt less alone in their pain. Just as Christ had healed many people from physical infirmities, he also healed these sisters' hearts (See John 11).

Empathy is not a skill that only Christ possesses. It's a healing power we all possess.

BOUNDARIES

"Empathy is not empathy without boundaries" (Brown, *Gifts of Imperfection*). Boundaries are what is okay and what is not okay. That is very vague, and purposely so, because we all have different boundary needs. Those needs are a big topic I often address in my work. They are so important, but for most of us, they are also difficult. It's easy to feel like our boundaries are pushing people away or that we're being mean and selfish. When boundaries are established correctly, they allow us to love more abundantly.

I have another sister (yes, another one! I have four sisters in all) who was living with her in-laws. Over the space of a couple of years, she had her first two babies as things got more complicated in the house. There were other little cousins that were often coming over.

Grandma was at work during the day and Grandpa was around but often busy on the farm. My sister felt like someone had to take care of those kids and without being asked, she found herself feeding them, watching them, and cleaning up after them. After so long, this got frustrating for her, especially because no one asked her to babysit, nor did they thank her for doing so. Her frustration turned into resentment toward the kids and other family members. That made her even more frustrated because she knew the kids didn't deserve her resentment. They were just kids.

One day she learned about boundaries. She recognized that because she had no boundaries, it was hurting her relationships. So she changed her approach. Because she had two children of her own and lived in one wing of the house, she stopped taking responsibility for the other children. If she was needed, she would be willing to help, but people had to ask her. When she implemented her boundary for this situation, she was able to love better in those relationships. She didn't like feeling frustrated with her family. She wanted to be kind and loving but found this boundary breach too much to handle. When she recognized the need for a boundary and gave herself permission to set it up, she felt unburdened by the frustration and could be more loving and kind.

Boundaries can be something small, like telling a roommate he cannot use your toothbrush. Or, they can be big, like telling your brother who has a problem with alcohol that he can't spend time around your kids until he gets sober. Either way, they allow us to respect ourselves and love those around us more authentically. As a therapist, there are natural boundaries that are set up to allow me to be empathetic freely. Many of these boundaries are ethical rules within my profession. For instance, I should not have "multiple relationships" with my clients. This means that I can't be a therapist to my neighbors or friends or anyone with whom I have an additional, pre-existing relationship. Ethically, that allows me to be more objective so I can do my job well. Another boundary I use personally is to minimize contact with clients "after hours." When I am fielding calls and messages in the evenings and on weekends, it becomes too much and takes me away from my family. There have been times I break that

CHAPTER 7: VULNERABILITY, EMPATHY, AND BOUNDARIES

boundary. I own it and take responsibility for when that breach has negative consequences.

Boundaries are important but also difficult. Most important things are super hard! I've seen some students make the difficult choice to tell their divorced parents it is not okay to talk negatively about either parent to them. Parents see the children as confidants and rely on their support. But the children are burdened all the time and feel responsible for their parents' emotions and biased in their love for each parent. They want to be free to love both parents without the feeling of being disloyal.

There have been times I've seen people put up a boundary that they cannot spend too much time with certain family members because those members are unable to be respectful. That is a hard thing to do and a hard thing to maintain. I often say that when a new boundary is being built within a pre-existing relationship, "You have to build it and reinforce it with sandbags." Sometimes people will try to push it over. This usually means multiple conversations about the boundary. However, most people respect boundaries, especially when they are explained in a way that communicates love. There may be an adjustment phase, but most meaningful relationships will indeed adjust. If they cannot, either the boundary needs to be reassessed or distance maintained as the next boundary.

When it comes to building new boundaries and the conversations required, it is important to lead with love. For example, with divorced parents, it could go this way: "Mom I need you to know how much I love you and care about our relationship. It is so important to me to feel close to you. So I need you to know that when you talk to me about how much Dad frustrates you and how you hated being married, it makes me frustrated with Dad. I think about how he did all those bad things and it makes me frustrated with you for telling me all those details. I start to feel resentful toward you. These conversations do not allow me to feel close to you. I love you and want to feel love, not frustration."

It can be difficult for Christians to find the balance between being charitable and loving versus being overused and taken advantage of. We are told to love and serve always, which is a good principle. What we are not taught is how to love and serve in ways that include boundaries and priorities and self-respect. That balance is especially hard to find when fulfilling leadership roles. Sometimes we believe it's our duty to do everything possible to serve, even when it might negatively affect our family and relationships. I remember my mother telling me of a time when she held a very high demanding church position. Boundaries were not my mother's strong suit. She felt that if she said no, she wasn't being a faithful servant.

One night, a family was in need and my mother did not know how to help. She felt a strong need to help but didn't have time to make a separate meal. So, she took them the meal she had made for our family. That choice caused contention between her and my dad. He was very supportive of her in her church involvement, but he was not supportive of putting everyone else's needs before our family's. That was taking it too far. The scripture does not tell us to "Love one another and sacrifice your own needs and the needs of your family in order to do it." It's okay to take care of our needs and the needs of our family first. When I say needs, I don't only mean temporal and tangible needs. Sometimes we can sacrifice too much emotionally and have nothing left to give those who matter most. There may be days when we can go out and serve and help someone, but emotionally we need to stay home and take care of ourselves or just take a break. Yes, take a break, people! Stay home, take a bath, and snuggle someone you love, or in a cozy blanket by yourself, if that is what you need.

Again, identifying core values will help in the building or maintaining of boundaries. Boundaries are necessary to live in line with our integrity. Those things we are holding onto or pushing back against that are not involved with our values, and we just can't let go. Boundaries protect our values. Boundaries should not protect our fears or insecurities.

Even Christ had boundaries and needed a break. In the New Testament, he is often "missing." He kind of runs away temporarily to seek alone time. He leaves the people and his disciples and goes out into the wilderness to commune with God. In some stories, he literally has hordes of people following him everywhere. Even for the perfect Christ of our world, that was tiring. He had to take a break and reconnect with himself and his maker. When I hear the story of Christ calming the storm in Mark 4, I laugh and cry. After a long

CHAPTER 7: VULNERABILITY, EMPATHY, AND BOUNDARIES

sermon, he decided to leave the multitude and take a boat across an inlet to the other side. He gets on the boat with his disciples and other people try to follow him in their own boats. He is literally being chased down by boats. It's like the paparazzi chasing down a big celebrity after a big concert. I think it's fair to assume that at times, Christ felt overwhelmed and even smothered. So while on this boat, Christ falls asleep. A sudden and terrible storm descends upon them and the disciples begin to be scared for their safety. I laugh because here this storm is so bad that the disciples feel like they are going to die, and Christ is sleeping. He must have been really tired! After all, he was still human and subject to fatigue like anyone else.

Christ was clear with his ethical boundaries. When he cleared the temple of all the people selling and making a profit off the traditions of the temple, he demonstrated boundaries. It was not okay for him to stand by and watch as people defiled the sacredness of the temple with their actions. He was frequently rebuking and speaking honestly with the scribes and pharisees as they tried to challenge and confound him. However, he still loved all those people and communicated his boundaries with kindness. In *Jesus the Christ*, James E. Talmage describes that "Jesus took up the malicious charge and replied thereto, not in anger but in terms of calm reason and sound logic" (Talmage, *Jesus the Christ*).

For me, the best indicator of a need to set boundaries is when I am starting to feel resentful toward an individual. Although that may not be a fail-safe method, resentment is a good signal that boundaries are either needed or being challenged. I want to feel close and connected to people, and if I notice my emotions turning resentful, I reassess to see if boundaries could help. Within my own self-awareness, I can assess if there is a need for more patience and charity, or if there is a need for boundaries. We have to be honest with ourselves because boundaries are *not* an excuse to serve and love less. If they are built in the right way, they allow us to serve and love more completely. For some, that may also mean serving less. When you do serve, it is a more sincere service.

I have a sister who has battled with that balance her entire adult life. Heidi has a lot of natural confidence, which draws people in. She gets along with all kinds of people, and it's easy to feel comfortable around her. She also has an eye to see people's needs and a heart to try to meet them. Possibly due to this, she has often found herself in unbalanced relationships. Her friends get used to her seeing and meeting their needs and start to take advantage of that. She put it this way:

> "It took a fairly long string of failed relationships with people before I saw this pattern:
>
> - Phase One: I meet someone new and invite them into my life;
>
> - Phase Two: We enjoy each other in the normal way friends do;
>
> - Phase Three: After some time, the new friend begins taking advantage of my kindness and I allow it, cheerfully;
>
> - Phase Four: I become silently resentful;
>
> - Phase Five: I feel the resentment built to the breaking point and I snap internally;
>
> - Phase Six: I pull away, making excuse after excuse until my friend finally leaves, hurt and baffled about why the friendship soured.
>
> "Once I realized this was the pattern with virtually every adult in my life, I knew I was the one with the problem, not everyone else. It was a revelation for me to learn that setting boundaries can be one of the most compassionate things I can do. What was once a badge of honor was revealed in its true light, the inability to say no. My understanding of Christlike behavior had led me to be a pushover rather than a minister. Someone once said, 'fountains attract drains,' and I had taken some pride in being the one to be the fountain.
>
> "I realized proper boundaries can give relationships space and a sense of safety. Everyone can relax and enjoy each other when they know where the boundaries are and where they are not. I continue to research and experiment with boundaries as part of my everyday life. It's not perfect. I still have to watch for those times when I feel resentment building.

CHAPTER 7: VULNERABILITY, EMPATHY, AND BOUNDARIES

"There is a risk, probably a normal one, for anyone on this kind of journey. As I have been trying to implement new boundaries, there is an element of loneliness. Where I used to be surrounded by people who acted like they loved and admired me, now I only have a few close friends who understand and respect me. I have had to reframe my need for social connection to be satisfied with these few but deeper friendships. It took some adjusting, but I admit that these relationships are far more valuable than the surface friendships I had been swallowed up in years ago."

PRACTICE

- Think of a time when you have been on the receiving end of empathy. Remember, empathy is not advice or suggestions. Empathy is "feeling with someone."

    o What did that change for you?

    o What did that change for that relationship?

- Have you had an experience when you have been on the giving end of empathy?

    o What did that change for you (this time for you on the giving side)?

    o What did that change for that relationship?

- What does your body feel like when you remember those experiences?

- Fill out the following chart:

Boundaries I have	Obstacles to the boundary	People who support the boundary	How I created the boundary

Boundaries I need	Obstacles to the boundary	People who would support the boundary	How to create the boundary

CHAPTER 8

Common Humanity

My husband and I had been married about a year when he told me he had a problem with sexual imagery and masturbation. In the extremely conservative culture and religion we were a part of, viewing of sexual images and masturbation were forbidden. There was a lot of teaching around avoiding these things to maintain sexual purity. This was similar to the purity culture that exists in many religious communities and religions. I debated whether or not to tell this story at all because so much of it hinged on purity culture, which was a huge part of the shame and struggle. There are loads to unpack within the context of purity culture, but I will save that for another time. I tell this story to illustrate common humanity, not to support a purity culture. When my husband told me for the first time, I remember it being really hard to talk about. I felt confused and my body was reacting to so many different emotions, but my brain didn't understand. Afterward, I felt hopeful that he had talked to me about it and "came clean." I naively thought, "Oh, how wonderful it is that my husband has been able to change this problem now and I won't have to worry about it ever again." Several years later, he admitted that it was still a problem and he had tried to handle it on his own—without success and without telling me. That time I felt more crushed than I thought possible.

I don't remember the specific conversation, but I do remember how emotional I was. I remember driving to work afterward and crying so hard that I realized I was being an unsafe driver. I had to pull over for a while until I calmed down a little. I had disillusioned myself so I thought that when my husband had confessed the first time, the struggle was over. This second time was like a blow with twice the force. I felt like the pain I was feeling would last forever. I worried I could never trust him again. I had thoughts that if only I was sexier and wanted sex more, maybe he wouldn't have this problem. In turn, that made me uncomfortable with intimacy altogether. I felt the need to monitor him all the time and constantly ask how he was doing. I felt mad that he didn't just stop. I felt more alone than at any other time in my life because I couldn't talk to anyone about it. I was desperate; so was he.

Based on the resources and information we had at the time, we were limited in our understanding of the issue. We did not know about positive sexual development and how to view the behavior with less shame. All we knew was "feel shame about it and just stop it." That was the method. In my years of experience working with clients with similar problems, the "just stop it" method doesn't work with anything. Yet, I didn't know then what I know now. I hadn't even started grad school at that point. What I strongly believed was that sexual imagery and masturbation were bad.

The main treatment option we had was a 12-step group patterned after Alcoholics Anonymous (AA). My husband started attending and got a lot out of it. It did not necessarily change the problem, but he had a safe place to talk and felt supported by other caring individuals. This is why support groups and other 12-step programs are so successful. They create an environment where people are welcomed and able to share without judgment. As he attended, we learned there was a support group available for the wives. My husband suggested I go. I wanted so badly to have a place to talk and was excited to go. But coupled with the excitement was uncertainty. The biggest problem with purity culture is shame. The second biggest problem is that no one wants to talk about it. The idea of meeting with a group full of people I didn't know, where I was supposed to reveal our "deep dark secret," was terrifying. I went anyway.

I walked into the room and there were about thirty chairs placed in a large circle. Some women were already sitting, talking quietly. They

CHAPTER 8: COMMON HUMANITY

greeted me with kind expressions. In that instant, things changed. I realized these women were there for the very same reason I was. I was no longer walking to this gloomy confessional, I was among friends. When we saw each other, even though I didn't know them, there was an instant connection. We knew we shared the same pain. I'm sure that they saw the same initial fear in my face that they'd felt personally. Their intent was to replace my fear with love and acceptance.

Without even exchanging words, we knew each other in a more sincere way than I knew some of my lifelong friends. As I sat, the room continued to fill with other women until nearly all of thirty chairs were taken. There was a facilitator who led us in reading the step in focus that week. We went around the room as women took turns sharing any thoughts, ideas, or experiences that were relevant to the step. The feeling of connection I had upon entering the room continued to grow as I listened to each person talk. I don't even remember what I, or anyone else, said. I *do* know that when I left, I felt less alone and more hopeful about everything. The mere fact I was no longer alone in my experience started to heal my heart.

Since this experience, my understanding of sexual imagery and masturbation has evolved a lot. Personally and professionally, I am in a completely different place with how it is discussed, experienced, and treated. Yet, the value of sharing my vulnerability with those other women still remains powerful and important.

It is healing to recognize how we all suffer in some way. It's even more healing to join with others who suffer in similar ways. I can attest to the belief in common humanity, common struggle, and common shame. It is more real than any tangible thing you can hold in your hand. When we look at others with the understanding that they are the same as us, we can live a more honest and fulfilled life. There is less sorrow in loneliness and more celebration in connection.

When we can implement the idea that other people struggle, other people feel shame, and other people are stumbling through life too, we feel less resentment toward them. We're more likely to feel compassion toward them and ourselves. In *Daring Greatly*, Brené Brown tells a story about a conversation she had that started with her therapist and ended with her husband. Her therapist proposed the idea that "What if people are doing the best they can?" When later discussing the idea with her husband, he responded, "I will never know if people are doing the best they can or not, but when I assume that they are, it makes my life better" (Brown, *Daring Greatly*).

We really don't know what people are experiencing in their lives and how hard they are trying. That doesn't matter. It is not our place to judge and evaluate; it is our place to love, and loving comes easier if we recognize we're not the only one who suffers, struggles, and stumbles. We do not have the gift of perfect empathy as Christ did. He could see the person and the story all at once. Knowing the story is not as important as believing that there *is* a story. There is always a story. That is what makes us human. That is what helps us connect. It is a part of common humanity.

Using the term "common humanity" means the same thing as connection and having a sense of belonging. Brené Brown speaks to this:

> Belonging to ourselves means being called to stand alone—to brave the wilderness of uncertainty, vulnerability, and criticism. And with the world feeling like a political and ideological combat zone, this is remarkably tough. We seem to have forgotten that even when we're utterly alone, we're connected to one another by something greater than group memberships, politics, and ideology—that we're connected by love and the human spirit. No matter how separated we are by what we think and believe, we are a part of the same spiritual story. (Brown, *Braving the Wilderness*)

Frequently people have a different interpretation of a spiritual story. Pantheism is the belief that there is no one God as a separate entity but that all things in the universe are God. The universe and all that it includes contribute to the greater, all-encompassing God. It's similar to how we have specific elements like bones, a digestive system, and a nervous system that contribute to the body as a whole. The idea is that everything is connected because everything is God. For Christians, there are specifics within theologies that don't match up. However, Christians do share the belief that all people are connected as creations of God. The hymn, "How Great Thou Art," expresses the deep amazement for God when noticing the beauty he has created. The first verse

CHAPTER 8: COMMON HUMANITY

reads, "O Lord my God, when I in awesome wonder, consider all the worlds Thy hands have made; I see the stars, I hear the rolling thunder, Thy pow'r throughout the universe displayed." (How great thou art. https://genius.com/Religious-music-how-great-thou-art-lyrics.)

We belong to a human family and God binds us together. Whether it is a bond that is believed to be created through familial ties, or through an energy, we are bound to one another. Within our earthly families, there is a certain connection we can't change. That's why people who are adopted yearn to know about their birth parents, even if their relationships with their adoptive parents are solid and healthy. Or why estranged sibling relationships might hurt so much. Or how, even when a parent is abusive, the child often wants some sort of a relationship. Feelings of family connection exist on a larger scale, too. We get used to each other and get used to not knowing each other.

Melinda Gates said, "Connect deeply with others. Our humanity is the one thing that we all have in common" (https://www.quotelify.com/melinda-gates-quotes). When we believe in the value of common humanity, it creates natural compassion toward everyone as well as a better acceptance of self.

Pema Chödrön said, "Compassion is not a relationship between the healer and the wounded. It's a relationship between equals. Only when we know our own darkness well can we be present with the darkness of others. Compassion becomes real when we recognize our shared humanity" (Chödrön, *Places That Scare You*).

Compassion as a simple concept is easy to believe in. Most of us feel the need to be compassionate toward other people; however, we don't understand how that could have a direct influence on our introspection or view of self. If we believe that other people have value and deserve happiness, we have to include ourselves in that "people" demographic. We are not the one exception in the entire world.

In Kristin Neff's groundbreaking work on self-compassion, she suggests the idea of common humanity versus isolation. Neff explains that when people share their experiences and trials with others and they understand their pain, there is a connection that results in less suffering because the person is no longer suffering alone. On the flip side, when a person keeps themselves isolated in their experience, it makes the suffering worse (Neff, *Self-Compassion*).

I can't help but smile when I explain this because I am suggesting that even the vague idea of connection makes us happier. You don't actually have to create or engage in human connection. Yet, if you believe we are all connected by our shared experiences, you feel less pain. Amazing! And so very true.

In Buddhism, there is a well-known story about a mother and a mustard seed. A woman named Kisa Gotami had recently lost her only child, a son. She was so distraught and refused to accept his death. She traveled from house to house asking for medicines that could cure him. At one house, someone suggested that she find Buddha, who was traveling in the area, and ask if he could help heal her son. So Kisa found Buddha and pled with him to help. He told her that she needed to go collect mustard seeds from the houses in the village, only taking a mustard seed from each person who did not know death. Mustard seeds were a common ingredient in most households. Eager to follow his instructions, she went out to gather the mustard seeds.

She knocked on the first house and was greeted by a young boy. She asked the boy if she could have a mustard seed and he went to fetch her one. Upon his return, she remembered what Buddha had said. She asked, "Thank you, but I must ask if this house has seen death?" The boy replied, "Yes, my father died about a year ago and we miss him very much." Kisa said, "I appreciate your help but I cannot take this mustard seed."

So, she proceeded to the next house, with the same request. A kind, older woman brought her a mustard seed and Kisa again asked, "Has your house seen death?" The older woman responded, "Yes, my husband passed away eight years ago." Again Kisa replied, "Thank you for your help but I cannot take this mustard seed." And so she went on from house to house, asking about the seed and about death, never obtaining any seeds to take back to Buddha. After she had visited every house, she returned to Buddha with empty hands. She had also begun to understand that death was a part of life for everyone. She no longer needed help from Buddha because she was able to accept the death of her son.

This story illustrates that death is inevitable and that by accepting death, versus fearing and resisting it, we live with less suffering. However, when I first heard the story, I thought of connection and

CHAPTER 8: COMMON HUMANITY

common humanity. Kisa traveled to each house and spoke with people about their losses. It's a tender and vulnerable subject for anybody. I imagine that in those conversations, she felt compassion for the people she talked to. Maybe she stayed longer to listen to their stories and felt less alone in her pain. In those moments of connection and conversation, she learned to accept the death of her son. She also felt her heart heal because she was not alone in her sorrow.

This idea easily ties into our spiritual connection as children of God. When we view all people as children of God, it changes the way we interact. However, most of us have a hard time maintaining that perspective. Have you ever had an experience when you were quick to judge or acted poorly with someone then later found out that it was someone you knew but didn't recognize? I was pulling out of work one day and there was a car that cut me off. I honked and felt a little put off. As we both drove up to the stop sign, I began to worry that it was a client I had just finished a session with. I got anxious as I pulled up next to the car in the second lane. It was not my client, which was a relief, but my behavior got me thinking, "What if it was?" I had just finished a really powerful session. I care deeply about my clients, and my first priority is helping them feel loved and supported. How tragic it would have been if I had just finished a great, synergetic session with a client only to have them start driving and see me honk at them like a grouchy old woman!

I thought about how all people deserve that same consideration from me, not just those I work with. We all are bonded. We are all trying to get through life, however easy or difficult that may be. We are connected to each other. It is hard to recognize that in every moment. This can be easier if we ponder and try to value each person as a member of humanity, as a child of God. We will feel less alone in our struggle. Leonard Mlodinow said that "connection is such a basic feature of human experience that when we are deprived of it, we suffer."

During an interview, Maya Angelou said, "I believed that there was a God because I was told it by my grandmother and later by other adults. But when I found that I knew not only that there was God but that I was a child of God, when I understood that, when I comprehended that, more than that, when I internalized that, ingested that, I became courageous" (Brasted, "Interview with Maya Angelou").

Maya Angelou was a revolutionary woman who embodied the idea of being brave. Her first publication and most revered work was a memoir of her experiences as a young girl that included rape and murder resulting in her remaining mute for several years. This book, *I Know Why the Caged Bird Sings*, was published in 1969, a time when open discussion about sexual abuse wasn't happening. She dared to be vulnerable so she could help people heal. When she truly internalized what it meant to be a child of God, she could be more confident in telling her story, being vulnerable, living her dreams, and letting people see her full self, warts and all. In the same interview, she added, "When I was asked to do something good, I often said yes, I'll try, yes, I'll do my best. And part of that is believing if God loves me, if God made everything from leaves to seals and oak trees, then what is it I can't do?" (Brasted, *Interview with Maya Angelou*). The way she speaks demonstrates a unique amount of self-love and confidence. It is the complete antithesis of shame.

Practice

- Thinking back to Chapter One, what experiences have you had where you felt connected to others, even strangers? What was going on and how did your body and emotions feel?

- Sheri L. Dew stated, "None of us came to this earth to gain our worth; we brought it with us" (Dew, *No One Can Take Your Place*). Do you believe that statement? Why or why not?

- Many times I work with Christians who believe that all other people have infinite worth; however, they feel like they are the one exception in the entire world. They believe in the worth of everyone else but themselves. Do you feel you are the exception or the rule?

CHAPTER 9

Perspective and Unconditional Love

IN HIS BOOK, *7 HABITS OF HIGHLY EFFECTIVE PEOPLE*, STEVEN R. COVEY tells this story:

> I remember a mini-Paradigm Shift I experienced one Sunday morning on a subway in New York. People were sitting quietly—some reading newspapers, some lost in thought, some resting with their eyes closed. It was a calm, peaceful scene. Then suddenly, a man and his children entered the subway car. The children were so loud and rambunctious that instantly the whole climate changed.
>
> The man sat down next to me and closed his eyes, apparently oblivious to the situation. The children were yelling back and forth, throwing things, even grabbing people's papers. It was very disturbing. And yet, the man sitting next to me did nothing. It was difficult not to feel irritated. I could not believe that he could be so insensitive to let his children run wild like that and do nothing about it, taking no responsibility at all. It was easy to see that everyone else on the subway felt irritated, too. So finally, with what I felt was unusual patience and restraint, I turned to him and said, "Sir, your children are really disturbing a lot of people. I wonder if you couldn't control them a little more?"
>
> The man lifted his gaze as if to come to a consciousness of the situation for the first time and said softly, "Oh, you're right. I guess I should do something about it. We just came from the hospital

where their mother died about an hour ago. I don't know what to think, and I guess they don't know how to handle it either."

Can you imagine what I felt at that moment? My paradigm shifted. Suddenly I saw things differently, I felt differently, and I behaved differently. My irritation vanished. I didn't have to worry about controlling my attitude or my behavior; my heart was filled with the man's pain. Feelings of sympathy and compassion flowed freely. "Your wife just died? Oh, I'm so sorry. Can you tell me about it? What can I do to help?" (Covey, *7 Habits of Highly Effective People*)

This story is a great illustration of how quickly our emotions and judgments change when we have more information. For Covey, his irritation with the children and the false judgments of the father immediately changed when he heard the whole story. That change allowed him to access empathy for this family. We increase our ability to be kind and to connect when we have more information.

I was working with a young man named Ryan. He had mastered the art of resentment. He was resentful toward so many different people that his entire worldview was angry and jaded. In one session, we were talking about a mission he went on for his church. It was a common custom for the young men to do in his Christian culture. When I heard him talk about his mission, it seemed like he hated it. In reality, he did hate many parts of it but not all of it. He was paired up with another young man and they worked together all the time. One day we began talking about his companion. The relationship had soured early on and the two barely talked. They would do their work, and all the time in between was spent in silent resentment of each other. I started to ask more about this companion, but my client had very little to tell.

Because they had offended each other and took opposite sides of the "ring," they never got to know each other. By this time in my sessions with Ryan, he had come a long way with his self-awareness. He understood that his jaded and skeptical behavior in relationships was not always received well. He had a parent diagnosed with schizophrenia, and as a result, Ryan armored himself against pain but also vulnerability and connection. His hard exterior was not only hard to

CHAPTER 9: PERSPECTIVE AND UNCONDITIONAL LOVE

receive, but it caused Ryan to view many people as cruel, like his companion. Ryan genuinely thought his companion was heartless.

As well as doing hefty self-reflection work, we tried to better understand this companion. It was telling to me that Ryan didn't know many personal details about him. That also made it hard to guess any of the companion's emotions. So I offered a possibility. I said, "What if your companion came from a broken home? Maybe his parents were no longer together and he had to learn early on how to take care of and protect himself. He also had to provide a lot for the rest of the family. (Ryan's companion was a native from the area, a poor South American country, so the idea that he experienced poverty was very possible.) On top of all this struggle growing up, he was sexually abused by his uncle as a kid, and as a result, he does not trust other males very easily. He has to defend himself against any mistreatment and feels threatened emotionally." My guess was just that, a guess.

After considering this detailed possibility of his companion and recognizing struggles and experiences similar to his own, Ryan felt a shift from resentment to understanding. He also struggled with trust and was always on the emotional defense. He knew that those behaviors were not serving him well, but that was all he could do to get from day to day. Possibly, his companion was doing the same thing. Trying his best to survive. When we know very little about people, it makes it easy to assume incorrectly based on the limited evidence we see. A change in perspective can alleviate frustration and pain. Understanding others better is a self-serving practice because of what it does for us.

Here is an analogy for Harry Potter fans. For anyone who might not know, Harry is a young wizard and most of the books depict his experiences at the Hogwarts School of Witchcraft and Wizardry. As an infant, he was nearly killed by the evilest wizard of all, Lord Voldemort. In every book/movie, Harry is continuing his fight against this villain. At Hogwarts, there is a Professor named Severus Snape. Snape has a dark countenance and from the very first book, he seems to loathe Harry. Harry and Snape interact in various ways throughout the books, but there is always an air of disdain between the two of them.

Readers and viewers can easily assume the worst in Snape. He seems to be jaded and callous without reason. (Spoiler alert ahead! Skip the next couple of paragraphs if you don't want to know a part of the conclusion of the series.) In the last book, Harry learns more about Snape's story. Snape was best friends with Harry's mother and had always loved her. However, Harry's father would tease and bully Snape. With Snape's dying breath, and by magical means, he tells Harry the whole story. After Harry's mother died, Snape vowed to always look out for and watch over Harry, but he would only do it on the condition that Harry would never know what happened between him and his parents. So the act of disdain cloaked what was love and protection.

For many Harry Potter fans, once the full story of Snape came out, there was a newfound loyalty to Snape. All those Snape haters became Snape superfans. They found new meaning in all of the anger and harsh words. Snape's life of dark gloom was seen as sorrow and pain. He essentially died protecting the child of the love he never had. Fitting, I suppose, because it is a British tragedy.

In sessions, I spend a lot of time talking about perspective and how that can make a positive shift in the way we view others and in the way we view our relationships and experiences. It is helpful to try to view a situation through the lens of shame to understand another's perspective. This is especially useful with parent/child relationships. Most parents are operating from a place of love, however unseen or misunderstood that may be to the child. I have heard shocking things that parents say and do to their children. At times, I have to check myself to make sure I am not just jumping to the assumption that the parent is hateful and spiteful. In reality, those shocking and hurtful things source from the parent's shame. This is a more complete perspective of the parent's story and behavior.

One story often heard is about a mother who is overly critical of her daughter regarding weight and appearance. Parents will sometimes say things that are not at all okay like, "You are getting fat." "You shouldn't be eating that because you will gain weight." "You look ugly in that." Or, my personal favorite, "A girl who wears glasses will never

CHAPTER 9: PERSPECTIVE AND UNCONDITIONAL LOVE

get a boyfriend." If I'm working with a client who has heard things like this from their mother, I immediately want to learn more about the mother. Without exception, there is more going on for the mother that contributes to her harsh remarks.

In grad school, I did a research project on body image. The only thing I remember from that assignment was this statistic: The main indicator of risk for low body image for a girl is the low body image of her mother. Those attitudes are learned. So when a mother says to her daughter, "You look fat and should go on a diet," it is coming from a place inside her that says, "I look fat; I need to go on a diet."

The mother's poor behavior is a deflection of her own shame. She is projecting her own insecurities onto her daughter and, in a way, that helps her avoid her own "You are not good enough" discomfort. This is a clear example of shame deflecting. This can also be seen with harsh punishments. A parent can be overly harsh with consequences when a child misbehaves as a way to avoid the pain that their shame creates. They think, "When my children misbehave, it is my fault. I should have taught them better." Deflecting that shame results in more punishment. I have been that parent. Not okay.

Another example is when a parent is not responsive to the emotions of a child. They tell the child to "suck it up" and "get over it." This might stem from a lifetime of experience where emotions only cause pain, and it seems better to avoid them altogether.

Please note that this change in perspective is *not meant to excuse bad behavior*. This is not a place to justify bad things done or said. However, when there is more understanding of the story behind the behavior, there is less pain for the children involved. When a daughter can recognize that when Mom makes mean comments on the daughter's appearance, that is sourcing from a place of shame for the mom. It is more about the mom than it is about the daughter, which means it is *not true*. This allows those hurtful experiences to hurt less. Such understanding takes a lot of practice, especially in our most important relationships, like family. We are more sensitive to pain with family. Like in Covey's story, when we can see more of the full picture, we can access our unconditional love.

Unconditional Love

When we talk about unconditional love, there is often an unclear understanding of what that really is. We say we will always love someone, but if we are honest with ourselves, there are some requirements for that love. I have a sister who, for a long time, was conflicted with her religion. She went back and forth between believing and leaving for years. She was married quite young. It was a quick engagement and the beginnings of that marriage were rocky. In four years, she was divorced and letting go of her church. During this time, I was extremely devout and personally had a really hard time accepting what she was going through. I would have conversations with her about how she didn't believe anymore. It would make me mad because I grew up looking to her as an example of faith. When she was in high school, I saw her as this spiritual giant. I loved and appreciated her faith so much. To hear her deny something I felt to be so meaningful, well, I couldn't help but feel like she was lying. I thought she just wanted attention or wanted to be different. I still loved her as a sister, but I could not find a place in my heart to understand and accept her. My love was conditional.

Obviously, that put a huge strain on our relationship. We didn't really talk for years. It wasn't a deliberate avoidance; however, our lives had gone in such different ways that it took too much effort to connect. The next five to eight years were full of great struggles for my sister. Difficult relationships, another divorce, addiction, job changes, and extreme family tension. Looking back, all I feel is sorrow and compassion for her. She was very alone during this time and had less-than-ideal support from me and our family. I remained frustrated far too long. I would think, "Just stop making these bad decisions and your life won't be like this! Isn't it obvious?" I felt like she had the answers to feel more joy and was deliberately ignoring them. I was wrong. She was trying her very best to get through. Her shame was working hard and doing a lot of damage. Also, her perspective on faith and God was different from mine. She did not have the same meaningful experiences I did.

Over time, things changed. She changed. I changed. I got married at about the same time she had her first divorce. I started having

CHAPTER 9: PERSPECTIVE AND UNCONDITIONAL LOVE

children, which blew my mind with a perspective change. I remember after my first baby, I started looking at everyone around me and thinking, "Oh my gosh! He is someone's baby! And so is she! And so are they! How did I not know that everyone is somebody's baby?" I went to grad school and learned better empathy skills. My sister was also making more of an effort to be with family and build those relationships. It wasn't all at once, but, gradually, I let go of the need to love her the way I wanted to love her. I started loving her anyway. I let go of judging her choices. I let go of her ever wanting to come back to the church (that was a big one). I let go of our differences. We built a mutual respect for each other's boundaries and beliefs.

When I let go of those expectations, I found loving her to be the easiest and most fulfilling thing. She was, and always has been, a great person. All of her positive qualities got deserved attention. Because I no longer focused on our differences, I found a beautiful place in our similarities, of which we had tons. I had more interests in common with her than anyone else in my family. Currently, I am very close to her and that connection is simply founded on real, untouchable love. For all those years, I thought I loved her, though we didn't really get along. She was my sister. Of course I loved her. But that love was trapped within specific parameters with expectations and judgments, so it couldn't grow. That love was like Japanese foot binding—completely wrapped and compressed in order to avoid growth while simultaneously causing enormous pain.

Years later, I found myself in the midst of my own spiritual deconstruction. I was seeing my sister in a new light and, ironically, she was one of the first people I turned to for support. Something I neglected to give her. She did not judge or push any of her perspectives onto me. I was open and honest about my experiences. She was open and honest about hers. She empathized. We connected deeply while on a canoe in the middle of a beautiful mountain lake, which was incredibly healing for me.

I was talking to a friend who has a gay son. I was curious about how he had moved through that situation and how his relationship with his son had been affected. He said that it took a while at first, but the most healing part for him, his wife, and their son came when they let go of everything else and just loved him. Let go of religious doctrine, let go of a specific view of what happiness is, and let go of needing or wanting anything different for him. They just loved him. It changed their experience and their relationship for the better. I know when I loved my sister fully, that invited her to love me fully as well. Complete, unconditional love strengthens the bonds on both sides.

Christians from all different sects believe in loving one another. But do we? I know that, for too long, I didn't. Many times, when I would think I wasn't judging people, there was still a part of me that was putting them in a "less than" category because of their choices and differences. I would still be kind, but I'd keep part of my heart closed. I had the faulty thinking that if I *really* loved and accepted them, I'd also be approving of their choices. That's not true. Acceptance is not the same as approval. The resistance to fully accept others keeps our love from being whole. I have seen this happen in families. I've talked to mothers and fathers who feel that if they fully accept their children, they're letting go of the hope that they'll change in the ways they want them to change. They also feel responsible for the choices of their children. So, not only do they hope their child will change, they hope that all their efforts as parents will create that change. Parents feel responsible, which triggers their shame. Alas, shame wins again! Shame convinces parents they are responsible for the actions of their children. So, if children choose differently from what their parents have taught, it must mean the parents have failed.

This kind of hope for conformity and the feeling of responsibility can be scary and sad. Real hope, however, is not to be placed in the children and what they will or will not do someday. Hope is to be placed in God. Our responsibility is to do our best and love. As my friend with a gay son said, "You can't pray away agency." I would add that you can't pray for change you assume is needed for them. Your assessment of the need for change may not be what they really need.

In the book, *Their Eyes Were Watching God*, a character named Janey says, "Two things everybody's got tuh do fuh theyselves. They got tuh go tuh God, and they got tuh find out about livin' fuh theyselves." Evaluate your love for those around you. Are you holding part of that love back? If they never change, can you love them anyway?

A story that depicts Christ's boundless love is found in a surprising setting, starting in John, Chapter 13. Christ had been traveling,

CHAPTER 9: PERSPECTIVE AND UNCONDITIONAL LOVE

preaching, and healing for a very long time. He was investing so much of his time and care in teaching the disciples. He needed them to carry on his work after he died. They meant so much to him. They were all preparing for their last meal together. Christ wanted to make the most of this last chance to teach. For the next four chapters of scripture, he does teach. This is where the sacrament ordinance began, one of the most important practices in most Christian religions. However, Christ was saddened. He wanted to make this a special moment, but he knew that he had already been betrayed by Judas. By this time, Judas had already promised to deliver Christ to his enemies after the supper. Christ seemed rather sullen for a while, but at no time did he directly rebuke, or even call out, Judas. So many emotions must have been contending within Christ. He is facing his death and wanting to teach all the most important final things. He will miss his friends, and one of those dear friends has been playing a great part in sending him to his death.

Christ teaches them about the symbolism of his body and blood through the partaking of bread and water. Then he washes the disciples' feet. As he washes them, he says that the disciples were "clean every whit: and ye are clean, but not all." That was a subtle way to share his knowledge of Judas. After he finishes washing, he begins to preach. Then, the emotion of the betrayal gets to be too much. We learn "he was troubled in spirit, and testified, and said, Verily, verily, I say unto you, that one of you shall betray me." Still, he does not point out Judas directly. This sends the disciples into a frenzy, wondering who would betray their Master. As Simon Peter was leaning on Christ, he asked quietly, "Lord, who is it?" Jesus answered, "He it is, to whom I shall give a sop, when I have dipped it." This was a customary practice to dip bread in a sauce or gravy and hand it to another person. So Christ dipped the bread and handed it to Judas. That was as direct as Christ would be because he still loved Judas (John 13:26).

As he took the bread, the scriptures say, "Satan entered into him." Now, I believe that to mean when Judas took that bread, he knew that Christ knew. At that moment, their eyes probably locked and Judas was overwhelmed with shame (something that comes from Satan, for sure). As we know, shame can make us feel and act many different ways. Judas could have been very angry, as anger is a way to deflect shame. He could have felt more humiliated and ashamed. What was most beautiful was what Christ said next.

He could have reacted in so many ways. He was in the moment of accusation. Still deeply loving Judas, he simply said, "That thou doest, do quickly." Judas quietly left. Christ did this in such a way that the other disciples didn't even know the meaning of his words. They may have just assumed Judas was running an errand for Christ. He didn't want to make it obvious. There was already too much pain. Publicly inflicting pain on Judas would not make it any better (John 13:27).

Afterward, Christ starts to minister to the disciples. He starts to talk about love and tells them, "A new commandment I give unto you, that ye love one another; as I have loved you, that ye also love one another. By this shall all men know that ye are my disciples, if ye love one to another" (John 13:34). I think he is specifically talking about Judas. He knows that all will be revealed soon enough and the other eleven disciples will know what Judas did. Christ wants them to still love him. To be known best as a disciple, they must love. Gosh! I can't help but be in awe and wonder about this. We hate Judas! He has been on the "top ten most hated Bible bad guys' list" forever. But Christ never wanted that. Right after he addressed and dismissed Judas, he started talking about love. Love for everyone! Honestly, when I read these passages and really understood the love and sorrow of this story for the first time, it made me cry. Still does. We can all feel that kind of unconditional love, even when our heart is broken.

If you google the definition of "perspective," the first option says perspective is "the art of drawing solid objects on a two-dimensional surface so as to give the right impression of their height, width, depth, and position in relation to each other when viewed from a particular point" (https://ermer.weebly.com/perspective.html). Although this is an art concept, it provides a great emotional metaphor. To see people with a better perspective is an art as well. It is taking something (or someone) that looks one way and creating a more accurate impression of the full picture. Being a therapist gives me daily opportunities to practice perspective. People share their most vulnerable pains, emotions, and experience. I know it is a special privilege to take part in this process. Outside of work, I still see people as I see my clients, meaning I see most people as humans with deep emotions, tender

CHAPTER 9: PERSPECTIVE AND UNCONDITIONAL LOVE

hearts, and lonely sorrows. I have often found myself wishing more people could experience what it's like to be a therapist. As odd as that sounds, I feel like it would change so much in this world. I am better able to deal with my shame as a wife and a parent because I love my clients. My life is better because I regularly get to see all of a person and love them completely. This is a gift that gives me a small understanding of how Christ views us all.

Christ gets it. We will never have that natural understanding of man as He has. However, that doesn't mean we can't broaden our minds and open our hearts in ways that allow our perspectives to change. We may not know the exact story or struggle, but we are wise to assume that there is a story. This change in perspective and invitation to love creates the connection we crave.

Practice

- Identify a person in your life who has hurt you or is difficult to connect with. (Be cautious with your choice. Don't jump to the most painful relationship yet.)

- Create a possible story that might contribute to his or her behavior.

- Reflect on the story you created and see how that makes you feel about the relationship, the person, and yourself. Is it any different?

- Is there a relationship in your life where your love is restricted?

- What are you holding out for with that love?

- What is that resistance hurting?

- If you let it go, what would that change?

CHAPTER 10

Mindfulness

MINDFULNESS HAS BECOME A COMMON BUZZ WORD IN PSYCHOLOGY in the past eight to ten years. Ironically, it is a method and practice that out dates any modern psychological treatment. It seems that the wisdom of old was centuries ahead of the research. We are just now catching up. Mindfulness is something we experience and practice individually. When we are more mindful, individually, we usually reduce the suffering in our experiences and our relationships. Studies suggesting the benefits of mindfulness are not hard to find and provide empirical evidence supporting better wellness and satisfaction—physically, emotionally, mentally, and especially spiritually. The roots of mindful meditation began as spiritual practices. I use mindfulness with nearly every one of my clients. It is especially helpful with anxiety and also very effective when dealing with depression, stress, PTSD, addiction, OCD, and everything in between. I have even used it with couples.

So what is mindfulness? Jon Kabat-Zinn, one of the leading names in the American mindfulness movement, says, "Mindfulness is awareness that arises through paying attention, on purpose, in the present moment, non-judgmentally . . . and then I sometimes add, in the service of self-understanding and wisdom" (Kabat-Zinn, et al., *Mindful*). Some of you may say to yourself, "Sure, that is clear as mud." To which I say, "I know, I felt the same way." Mindfulness is a practice as well as a concept and a way of being, so it's hard to define.

When I introduce mindfulness to clients for the first time, I say it can start with a deliberate focus on something simple like breathing or physical sensations, and by so doing, you are not giving the anxious and worried thoughts a turn. It can be a nice break from the regular demands of life as well as a restart for your body and mind, like rebooting a computer.

Have you ever had days or moments when you feel more quiet and calm and you seem to be more aware in general? In those times, do you see yourself less reactive to regular life stimuli? That is what being mindful feels like. It is not being silent and sad or angry or any other strong emotion. It is a sense of quiet, calm, and awareness. When we are mindful, we are better able to deal with regular stressors and stay more in touch with ourselves and our surroundings. Sometimes this happens naturally. Other times, it is a state of being that we cultivate and practice with intention.

Breathe

The practice of mindfulness can be many things. For beginners, I start them out with basic meditation and breathing exercises. Deep breathing is deliberately inhaling and exhaling as much as possible. Allowing the breath to travel all the way into the bottom of the belly and not just the chest. When we are anxious and stressed, our breath is shallow and quick. That makes the anxiety worse because our bodies are getting less oxygen. Oxygen depletion can cause all sorts of problems like light headedness, muscle tension, nausea, and headaches. If you think about it, our bodies naturally take deep breaths as a way to calm the body. How many times have you finally laid down in bed after a long day and taken a deep breath in and out? You are preparing to fall asleep and releasing all the tension from the day. Or, we see it on TV all the time: a performer takes a deep breath before going out on stage, a boy takes a deep breath before he talks to a cute girl, or an athlete takes deep breaths before the race. Deep breathing is the first approach to calm.

There are many different breathing practices. Anything intentional and deeper is valuable. I prefer belly breathing. Belly breathing is focusing on moving the abdominal muscles in and out with each breath. For many of us, our abs don't move with breathing. We are diaphragmatic breathers, meaning the breath remains in the diaphragm. Research shows that when the full belly (abdominal wall) moves, it triggers the vagus nerve which is linked to the parasympathetic nervous system—our "calm system." Here is how I teach it:

> I want you to close your eyes and listen to me count. I'm going to pick some numbers to count to but I may change them as we go. Everyone has different lung capacities and the objective is to breathe in as deeply as you can, pushing your belly all the way out, and then exhale as far as you can while deflating the belly. Always exhale longer than you inhale. We will start with five seconds breathing in and seven seconds breathing out. Remember to breathe slowly.

Then I count for several minutes as they breathe. Five seconds for the in-breath and seven seconds for the out-breath. If I can tell they are needing more or less time for each breath, I adjust the numbers. Some people (especially musicians, swimmers, and singers), have very high breath numbers. Others are usually in the five to seven or six to nine range.

There is a great deal of interesting research on breathwork right now. If you google "benefits of breathing," you'll find all sorts of results and a long list of benefits. Interestingly, "remaining alive" was not found on any list. I assumed that would be number one. If you think about it, breathing is our most basic function of life. When it is done well, it enhances everything else. We release body toxins and muscle tension, boost our digestive, nervous and immune systems, and on and on. There is even a study that found evidence that proper breathing through your nose contributes to more symmetrical and attractive facial features. Healthy breathing makes us beautiful people (Bianchini, Guedes, and Vieira, "A Study on the Relationship between Mouth Breathing and Facial Morphological Pattern").

On Easter, a well-known mountain alpinist and ski mountaineer named Janelle Smiley posted on one of her social media accounts. She, her husband, and several other alpinists were skiing across the entire Alps mountain range in Europe. "The connection our spirit has to our bodies is held by our breath. If our breath stops then our spirit is no longer bound by our bodies. This concept has captured my mind lately. I am so grateful for Him who gave His breath so we could fully live the divine breath through our bodies" (Smiley, Instagram). The awesome power of breath is a divine gift.

Mindfulness Practice

After we have a good understanding of deep breathing, I go on to do mindfulness with them. There are many different styles of mindfulness practice. It is something that can be done anytime, anywhere, and by anyone. I prefer to start with a body scan, and I usually use or give a guided meditation. Guided meditation is when the meditator is listening to someone verbally walk them through different things to focus on and pay attention to. I do this myself, or at times I use guided meditations from other sources, like apps (there are many great apps with a variety of meditation options and resources). The body scan covers the whole body, head to toe, by slowly and deliberately focusing on different areas of the body and the sensations associated with that area. You go from the top of the head down to the tips of the toes. As you slowly move from one area to the next, you notice different textures, temperatures, tension, body positions, pressure, or any other sensations available. This is something that can be done in three to five minutes. To experience the full benefit of the practice, it should be ten minutes or longer. And if you are detailed in your focus, paying attention to every small area, it can easily go beyond ten minutes. Here is an example of the face portion of a body scan:

> Start with placing your focus on your forehead. Is there any tension? Don't change it, just notice it. Do you feel any specific temperature or other sensations like hair touching the skin or dry or tight areas of the skin? Now, move your focus to the temples. How do they feel? Are there any specific sensations associated with that area? Move to the eyes. How does it feel to have your eyes closed? Do you feel any pressure against your eyelids? Are your eyes relaxed or tense? Are there any other sensations around your eyelids or eyelashes? Shift your focus to the nose. How does it feel to breathe in and out? Notice the difference in sensation with every in-breath

versus every out-breath. Does the temperature change? Do you feel the air inside your nostrils? What is that like? Now, shift your focus to your cheeks. Are they tense or relaxed? Is the skin dry or normal? Can you feel any other sensations in that area? Focus on your mouth. What is the position of your lips? How do they feel? Tense? Relaxed? Dry? Moist? What about inside your mouth? What taste do you notice? Is your mouth wet or dry? Move your tongue around and notice how your teeth feel. Shift focus to the jaw area. Is there tension in the jaw? Is your jaw clenched or hanging? What is that like? Finish by focusing on your chin. What sensations are involved with that area? Is there a specific temperature or tension? What does the skin feel like around the chin?

A body scan is a great place to start learning because the physical sensations are easily accessible and easy to focus on. Proficient meditators can sit and focus solely on their breath for a long period of time. That is not an easy place to start. I've been doing this for years and can't focus on my breath for more than thirty seconds. Maybe thirty-five seconds. The idea of mindfulness is being able to have that calm, directed focus with anything. Eating, walking, taking a shower, driving, listening to music. As you do those things, you are paying attention to small details as well as taking a slower, more thoughtful pace as you go. For instance, mindful eating turns into the most delicious experience ever. Mindful listening becomes a literal symphony of sounds, melodies, and instruments.

Throughout all of this learning and practicing, one thing is most important: no judgments. That means that as you are doing mindfulness, you cannot get caught up in judging anything about yourself, your practice, or your surroundings. That judgment will derail the whole experience. When I was talking about how I can only focus on my breath for thirty seconds, I am demonstrating negative judgment. Shame on me. (Actually no shame, obviously.) Be aware of what is happening. What will happen frequently, especially for beginners, is that the mind will often get distracted and wander off. That's okay. Don't judge that. Notice where your thoughts go and redirect them back. One hundred times if needed. This redirection is like taking a walk with a little toddler. If you have ever done that, you understand that the toddler will not be very good at remaining on the path. They wander all over. You have to kindly encourage them away from the road, off the neighbor's lawn, and around the pile of dog poop. You don't yell or start to judge them because they are toddlers. It's expected for them to wander. Judgment toward ourselves creates tension, distraction, shame, and ultimately resistance to the whole experience of mindfulness.

When getting better at not judging, there is a natural allowance and acceptance that takes place. You resist less and allow an honest experience to take place. Interestingly enough, that can still include discomfort. Take, for example, physical pain. I store all my tension in my shoulders. When I am stressed and anxious, my shoulders get tight and even rise. For me, that is a signal that I need to pay attention. While practicing mindfulness, I will notice that tension and stress. When I notice it, I can do one of two things:

1. Judge it and think things like, "Wow, Erika, you are stressed! You should be better at this. Let go of the stress. Let go of the stress. You are not letting go of the stress! You suck at this." That experience creates resistance, and resistance creates struggle.

2. I can accept the stress and tension in my shoulders and just allow it. I can become aware that I am stressed and accept it. I know it sounds counterintuitive, but by allowing it, I do not add resistance or more tension. My body can continue to relax and feel calm as well as my mind. I am not getting preoccupied with the stress. Accepting and allowing it helps the stress and tension be less painful.

There are several different theories on what the essential elements of mindfulness are. All theories include the principle of acceptance. Accepting the present moment, accepting our emotions, accepting our physical discomfort, accepting our relationships, and such. Acceptance is a powerful thing. When people accept their mental health disorders, there is less struggle. When people accept the death of a loved one, there is less sorrow. When people accept how their body looks, there is less discomfort. When people accept family members as they are,

CHAPTER 10: MINDFULNESS

without wanting to change them, there is less suffering. Some may say that acceptance can be a weakness. It's like accepting defeat or allowing weakness. However, acceptance is just letting go of the resistance to reality. It is an honesty move.

Non-judgment is another element of all mindful practices. It is not possible to fully accept something for which you harbor negative judgments. There can be honesty, "I have ADHD. I don't like that I have it, but it doesn't make me less of a person. I am still me." Or, "I have an addiction to a substance. It makes me sad and I hate myself at times. I am trying not to judge those emotions and accept the waves that come with addiction. I am loving myself along the way."

When Christ was crucified, there was a lot of physical pain and torture. He did not resist it. That would have made more pain and anguish. He accepted the experience, which may be hard to believe, but that created less suffering.

I was working with an amazing girl named Anna. She was coming in after the hardest nine months of her life. She described it this way:

> I will never forget the day I broke. It was February 20, 2018. I was sitting in class listening to my professor list off all of the assignments I had missed while I was in Colorado and what assignments were due the following week. I began feeling extremely overwhelmed. My mind was racing and I started to cry. I went out into the hall and sobbed to Joe on the phone. He calmed me down and I went about the rest of my day. I went to sleep and woke up the next morning totally stressed out and anxious. I know this may sound naïve, but that has never happened to me. I always wake up happy and fine, feeling capable.
>
> I will never forget waking up that next morning, completely helpless and hopeless. It continued. Morning after morning as the anxiety became crippling. It was immobilizing. I could not think. I could not eat. I could not make any choices. Everything was overwhelming. I was having thoughts I'd never had before. What the hell was going on? I was Anna! I was a perfectionist: the happiest, most capable, talented, successful, and outgoing person. Where did she go? I was confused. I was depressed. I failed two of my classes. I quit my calling. I stayed in bed most days. I couldn't see any light at the

end of the tunnel. My parents were so worried about me that they came up to talk about what was going on. I tried to explain myself, but I couldn't because I didn't know what was going on Nothing made sense. I had never experienced anything like it before.

The anxiety and depression got worse and worse. I didn't know who I was. I could barely function. The shame I inflicted upon myself was weighing heavy. I wasn't sure I could carry the burden for much longer. I went to a therapist in Salt Lake City and she diagnosed me with anxiety and depression. I couldn't believe what I was hearing. I'm sorry what? I have what? What is wrong with me? Where is Anna? Wait, wait. Does Anna have anxiety and depression? Are you sure you have the right girl?

Anna had been blindsided with extreme anxiety and depression. During this time, she also developed an eating disorder, which only compounded the struggle. She got to a point where the only way to move through it was to accept it. She continues:

This diagnosis began my journey on a new path I never thought I'd be on. Ever. It took some time for me to accept it. I was fighting and fighting and fighting my diagnosis for months. I didn't want it. I thought I would be weak if I accepted it. My pride held me back from admitting that I needed help. I was so broken and so lost and so scared. Despite my pride, I finally sought out all help. I could not imagine going one more day suffering the way I was. This step of self-acceptance was my first step on the path to recovery and healing. I didn't have to fight myself anymore. I finally chose to be on *my* side. I felt relief. Once I received help, my healing increased rapidly. I began learning things about myself and my situation. I learned that I am important. My mental and physical health are important.

When I really began to believe this, I saw a change in myself and my anxiety. I realized that there was nothing wrong with needing therapy, needing to take a break, or needing to be kind to myself. I was not a horrible person because I couldn't go 2,000 mph anymore. I learned to accept myself and my anxiety. Each day, I continue to accept myself more and more. This has come with patience and understanding. I do not judge myself or my anxiety.

Mindfulness and self-acceptance can help in so many ways. Mindfulness looks a lot like prayer. Prayer is something we are told we can do anywhere, anytime. It can bring us closer to God and help us feel more joy. There are many ways to pray. There isn't a wrong way. Traditionally, a lot of people sit quietly by themselves and try to focus on the words and ideas to communicate with God. During prayer, our minds often wander. If you are like me, there is an "autopilot" prayer going on a loop so whenever I start to think about other things, I have this other "background prayer" still playing. To be sincere and deliberate in our prayers, we need to kindly redirect our thoughts to the most meaningful thoughts we want to pray about. David O McKay once said:

> We pay too little attention to the value of meditation, a principle of devotion. In our worship, there are two elements: One is spiritual communion arising from our meditation; the other, is an instruction from others, particularly from those who have the authority to guide and instruct us. Of the two, the more profitable introspectively is meditation. Meditation is the language of the soul. It is defined as "a form of private devotion, or spiritual exercise, consisting in deep, continued reflection on some religious theme." Meditation is a form of prayer . . . Meditation is one of the most secret, most sacred doors through which we pass into the presence of the Lord." (McKay and Woodger, *The Teachings of David O. McKay*).

I have my own beliefs that I have about stillness and God. These beliefs are from the "Book of Erika." This book isn't scripture, doesn't get much attention, and it cusses a little, but I like it. I feel God is in us all. I believe there is a divine energy that connects all living things and that allows us to access greater wisdom and direction. This idea is not original, but it resonates with my experience of God. Some call it the spirit of God, inner voice, consciousness, our truth, the knowing, inner compass, or intuition. Some may argue the idea of a deity and personal knowing are different. I feel they are the same thing. I believe that when we are in tune with our core values and true inner self, that *is* God. This energy is not easily felt unless we are still. The business of life distracts us from God. If you pay attention to traditional spiritual practices all over the world, spanning any religion or culture, there are elements of stillness. We have to take time to be quiet and still so we can know ourselves and God.

We must also understand how mindfulness helps us connect and strengthen our relationships. As I have emphasized before, one of the biggest benefits of mindfulness is that it allows for less suffering. The principle of mindfulness starts as a deliberate practice where you meditate for a certain amount of time. The concept of being mindful translates into a way of being and a life perspective. There can be less suffering in all aspects of a person's life but especially in relationships. Psychologists call this "affect tolerance," which means the ability to tolerate or *be* with feelings. This helps us manage discomfort in our relationships and recognize the influence they have on us.

Being mindful makes us less reactive. When I am more mindful, I am more patient with my kids. Behavior that is normally triggering for me is not as overwhelming. When we find ourselves in hard places in relationships, mindfulness can help with our capacity to bear it. In sessions, I frequently talk about difficult relationships, whether it be families, spouses, roommates, coworkers, or friends. At times, in those situations, I come to a point where it is helpful to ask, "What if they never change? Could you let go of waiting for them to become the person you want or possibly deserve them to be, and find something good about the person they are now?" That is a really hard question to think about and, at times, it doesn't seem fair. But in those situations, when they can accept the present reality of their life instead of living in so much grief waiting for some unlikely change, they can find less suffering and more joy.

Mindful practice in marriage can help with the acceptance of our partners as well as help us manage our stress responses. I discussed the "Four Horsemen of the Apocalypse." These are negative behaviors that can be dangerous in a marriage. These behaviors (criticism, defensiveness, contempt, and stonewalling) are our stress response and often shame. When couples see these behaviors arise in themselves or their partner, they need to acknowledge the stress response and take a "time out" to deal with those emotions before returning to their partner. Again, stonewalling is one of my stress responses. I start to shut down

CHAPTER 10: MINDFULNESS

and get really quiet. Everyone can find their preferred method to "de-stress." For me, it is breathing and mindfulness. It helps me reconnect with myself and my emotions so that I can return to my husband and continue to work through things with him.

Mindfulness takes regular practice. It won't change you or your relationships overnight. Mindfulness is like a muscle. When we exercise our muscles often, they grow in strength and size. Our capacity to push ourselves increases and there becomes a perpetual positive benefit to the exercise. But when we stop, that momentum also decreases. In his *Great Courses* class titled "The Science of Mindfulness: A Research-Based Path to Well-being," Ronald Siegel talks about an experience he had while teaching at Harvard where he was privy to some rare and privileged face-to-face time with the Dalai Lama. During that conversation, Ronald learned that for the Dalai Lama to reach and maintain his level of awareness and mindfulness, he practiced four hours a day. That is incredible and highly unlikely for the rest of us to replicate. If we compare the Dalai Lama to an athlete preparing himself for a highly elite and rigorous event like the Ironman triathlon, then four hours a day is standard. The time-to-benefit ratio of mindfulness is not the same as exercise. We do not need to meditate for the same amount of time. However, some people do. Does that mean that regular exercise is only beneficial for the rest of us if we match that four hours? Of course not. That is an elite level of performance. We still experience immense benefits from regular exercise.

You have to find a good balance. Five minutes of running every day will not strengthen you as well as thirty minutes or sixty minutes. I once made a New Year's resolution to do mindfulness every day. By the second month, I had not missed a day. At that point, I asked myself if I felt different. Was there a positive change? The honest answer was no. I had been diligent with my practice, but sometimes my practice time was too short to create an obvious emotional difference. I recognized that to see positive change, I needed to practice longer. Many nights, I would only practice for five minutes. I told clients to practice for at least ten minutes and neglected to heed my counsel. In some cases, ten minutes may not be sufficient to help the body experience more peace and calm. Be honest with yourself. While four hours is probably too much, and thirty minutes may be unattainable at first, find a place that pushes you just enough but not too much.

The great thing about practice is that our skill improves. My "focus muscle" is stronger than it was when I first started years ago. Over time, I have discovered my personal preferences in my practice. For example, I have found that visualizing breathing in a cloud of air that is sucked in and out of my lungs with every breath helps me maintain better focus. Another common trick is to count breaths. One on the in-breath, two on the out-breath, all the way up to ten. Then I start over. There are specific kinds of meditation I do, depending on the mood I am in. When I am especially stressed and buzzing things around in my head, there is a meditation where I imagine myself near a river with fall leaves floating by in the water. With every passing leaf, I place one thought. I put my thought on the leaf and watch as it floats down the river. I do the same with my next thought and the next. It sounds simple, but it helps me sort, accept, and let go of my worries. On more calm days, I try simple breathing exercises. The great thing about mindfulness is that you can always improve and grow. It's not a practice that ever gets mastered. Accepting our inability to master anything is one of the main goals.

In Chapter Seven, I talked about how Christ is often found missing. When I read the New Testament, I often feel like he runs away. Not running away but seeking isolation to be apart from the people and his disciples so he can meditate and pray. Some examples are well-known, like the 40 days of fasting and his final prayer in Galilee. Other examples are easily missed. One example is in Mark 1:21-37. Jesus had been preaching in the synagogue all day. It was a busy day and afterward, he went to his disciple, Simon's house, probably to rest and eat. Once he got there, he learned that Simon's mother-in-law was very sick with a fever. Jesus healed her, and she started to minister to them. She had just witnessed a miracle and couldn't help but tell the whole village. So she did. She sent out the news and spread it all over the village. As the sun was setting, the entire town gathered at Simon's door, bringing their sick and diseased to be healed. After a long, busy day, Christ is presented with potentially hours of healing, helping, and loving. This probably goes well into the night.

CHAPTER 10: MINDFULNESS

That next morning, Jesus is not in his bed. Verse 35 says, "And in the morning, rising up a great while before day, he went out, and departed into a solitary place, and there he prayed." He needed to be alone. Every time he slips off to meditate, it doesn't last long before the people and his disciples find him. Of course, Christ, being who he is, returns and continues his work. So when Simon finds the empty bed, he searches for Jesus. When he finds him, he says, "All men seek for thee." Christ, after a night of little sleep and little time to recharge on his own, returns to preach and heal the people.

Another example of this is in Matthew 14. Jesus learns from his disciples that John the Baptist, Christ's dear friend and cousin, has been killed. Now, Jesus has a complete perspective of life and death and probably doesn't feel grief in the same way we do, but he still feels. There is a natural sorrow that happens when we lose loved ones, and I'm sure Christ was deeply saddened by the news. So he leaves with his disciples on a boat to get away, possibly to mourn. People learn that he is leaving, and they chase after him on foot. As Christ sees this multitude of people following him, he feels compassion and stops to teach and heal them. He preaches all day and the disciples say that everyone should take a break and return to their homes to eat. Christ, knowing the hearts of the people, instead wants to feed them himself. This is the feeding of the 5,000. After everyone eats, Christ sends his disciples away on the boat and sends the rest of the people away to their homes. Again, he is grieving after another day full of preaching and healing. No doubt tired and grieving, "he went up into a mountain apart to pray: and when the evening was come, he was there alone."

He likely needed space to breathe, mourn, and receive comfort from his father. Not surprisingly, that mindful time is cut short because while praying, he sees that the boat carrying his disciples is caught in a sudden storm. So again, being the loving man he is, Christ leaves his meditation to go save the disciples by walking on the sea.

As I have said before, mindfulness can be far more than a ten-minute practice you do before you go to bed. It can be done in so many different ways and become so much more than a practice. I've included more mindfulness exercises at the end of this chapter to provide more specifics on different ways to practice every day. I do not claim to be any sort of expert regarding mindfulness, which is why I am only touching on this topic briefly. There is a massive amount of information, research, books, apps, tutorials, and podcasts that can give you more direction and tools if you'd like to learn more. Although I'm not an expert in mindfulness, I do believe in its purpose. Not only is it something we can practice, but it can be a way of gaining more awareness in our everyday life. A way of living. When I do practice, even when I practice poorly, I still feel better. I feel greatly connected to myself, to life, and to God.

Mindful Practice Examples

These are examples of different ways to do mindfulness. Guided meditations are best done while listening. Here are some of my favorite apps that provide more options for meditations and mindful resources: Mindfulness Coach, Smiling Mind, Calm, and Insight Timer. Again, there is plenty of information that can assist you in your practice.

Mindful Eating

Mindful eating is done very slowly with a small amount of food. Some recommend eating something with a lot of texture, like crunch, to provide more observation; however, I like to do it with chocolate. Ultimately, it doesn't matter. Just choose something you can hold in your hand and something you like. First, you just observe the item. What it looks like and feels like. Then, you start to smell it and notice all the details of the aroma. Now, begin to taste just a little with the tip of your tongue. Notice what that does to your tongue and how your taste buds start to react to the flavor of that taste. Place a small piece of the food in your mouth; allow it to sit in your mouth without chewing or moving your tongue. Again, pay attention to what happens in your mouth as taste is experienced and saliva is released. Start to move the food around in your mouth, slowly. How does that feel? Start to chew slowly and notice what it feels like as you bite down. How does it feel to move your jaw in this way? Is there anything notable about that bite like sound, texture, or a new taste? Continue in this way until the food is gone. Once it is gone, what does your mouth feel like? Taste like? Is it dry or wet? Sweet or salty? Or, something else altogether? Mindful eating done right makes the food taste really good. You may notice that you don't like that particular food. You become so much more aware of all the flavors, textures, and the overall experience of eating.

Mindful Listening

This can be done listening to any sounds. I often recommend listening to music, preferably instrumental music. Begin by sitting in a comfortable, upright position or lying on the floor. Close your eyes and take several deep belly breaths. Start to listen and notice a soft awareness of the sounds. Start to pay attention to different details of the music. How many instruments can you identify? What sound is each instrument making? Are they loud or soft sounds? Notice the tempo of the music. Do the sounds rise or fall? Do the sounds remind you of anything? Are there any images or ideas that come to mind as you listen? How does your body feel while you listen? What is it like to receive the sounds in your ears? Can you feel that sound in your ears? Continue to breathe deeply, but naturally, as you listen to the whole song.

Mindful listening can be easier than other forms of mindfulness because there are so many sounds to choose from, and there are so many options for centering focus. The same principles of listening can be applied out in nature, while stuck in traffic, in the shower, or anywhere else. Apply deliberate observation of the sounds around you.

Mindful Walking

Find a place to walk where you have space and privacy. This can be a hallway or open area. It can also be outside. Make sure it is a place where you won't be overly distracted by other things. A long, empty hallway is a good place to start if you have never done this before.

Start out on one side of the hallway, or walkway, if you are outside. Take several deep breaths. Notice your breath as you stand. What does it feel like to breathe? Now scan through your body and get a general sense of how your body feels. Are you calm? Anxious? Are there strong sensations in your body that are easier to note? Tension, hunger, fatigue?

Shift focus to your legs and feet. How does it feel to support your weight on your legs and feet? Do your legs feel strong, tired, or neither one? How about your feet? Can you feel your body weight press on your feet? What is that like? Slowly lift one leg and take a step forward. Notice the sensation of starting with the foot on the ground to lifting it up with no pressure anymore to setting it down again and the pressure returns. Stop. What does it feel like with one step forward? How is your weight distributed? Now take another step with the other foot, noticing all the same sensations. Did one step feel different from the next? How? Keep taking slow steps and recognize the pressure of weight, the movement of the body, and the bending of joints. Notice different parts of the foot as you step. What muscles can you feel working in your legs and feet? Again, go very slowly so you can pay attention to different details.

This practice can continue as slowly or quickly as you like. It can be five minutes or thirty. As you continue to walk, you may notice your mind wandering or becoming distracted. Just as in any other mindfulness practices, notice where your mind wanders to and refocus back on the walking sensations.

Because your eyes will be open as you walk, it may be harder to maintain focus. That's okay. Continue to refocus. It may be helpful to take small breaks from focusing on the walking and allow your focus to shift to something else, like things you see or hear, or feel. Pick one of the five senses and spend time mindfully observing in that way. After a little time, shift your focus back on the walking.

If you reach the end of the hallway or walkway, turn around and go back. Repeat this as many times as you like.

Mindful Looking

This practice can be done by looking at any content such as pictures, nature, or people. Find a place to watch and observe without distraction. If you are looking at photos, make sure you can easily turn pages without too much movement. You want your body to remain as still as possible. It might help to spread the pictures out over a table so you don't have to move at all.

Start by taking deep breaths and allowing your body to settle into position. How does your body feel as you sit and breathe? Are there any strong sensations in your body? Subtle sensations? Place your gaze forward without focusing too much on any single detail. Pay attention to how your eyes feel. What is it like to see? Are there sensations in or around your eyes? Your head? Can you feel yourself blink? Shift your focus to something specific you can look at, anything around you. First, observe color. What kind of colors do you see? Are they bright or dull? Do you like any of those colors? Do the colors bring to mind any ideas? Start to observe shapes. What kind of shapes can you see? Are they large or small? Simple or complex? Are there shapes within shapes? Observe texture. Can you imagine how objects or areas would feel if you were to touch them? What does that texture make you feel or think? Lastly, observe how you feel looking at the pictures. Try not to fixate on the content as much as how your body feels while looking at them. Does that emotion change while looking from one thing to the next? Notice that emotion as you look.

Self-Compassion Mindfulness

Sit in a comfortable, upright position. Make sure your back is supported and your mind is alert. Start by taking several deep breaths in and out. Fill your lungs with as much breath as is comfortable. Slowly release the breath. How does it feel to breathe? How does it feel as the air enters and exits your body? Notice as you start to settle into your position and your body continues to relax. Think about people in general and all the struggles and emotional pain that people feel. Consider people from all over the world and the things they might be dealing with. Imagine how they might feel about those experiences. Think about the emotions they might be feeling. As you are thinking about these people, notice your own emotions. How does it feel in your body and in your heart as you think about these people? Start to cultivate compassion for them in your body. Notice what that compassion feels like. Where do you feel the compassion in your body? Focus on that sensation and let it grow. Send that compassion out to those people. Imagine that feeling passing from your heart to theirs. What does that feel like?

Bring to mind someone you know personally who has been having a hard time emotionally. Think about this person and how they might be feeling. What has been going on for them and how are they dealing with it? As you think about this person, how does it feel in your body? Start to cultivate compassion for them. Let it grow and build. When you are ready, send out that compassion to the other person. Imagine it moving from your body to theirs. What is that like? How would it make them feel? How does that make you feel? Shift focus to yourself. What emotional struggles have you had? What has that been like for you? Consider your own pain and struggle. What does that feel like to think about yourself this way? Cultivate the same sensation of compassion for yourself. Notice where you feel it and let it grow and build. When you're ready, allow your heart and body to absorb that compassion as if it were a healing balm absorbed through the skin to help your body feel better. Imagine that healing power of compassion entering your body. What does that feel like? Is there any resistance to absorbing it? Do you allow it? If you do, what does that absorption feel like? Let yourself notice and feel. Sit with that sensation of self-compassion for a moment, even if it is a small sensation. Sit and allow it to grow.

Other examples:

- Mindful driving/commuting
- Mindful showering
- Gratitude meditation
- Loving-kindness meditation
- Stress mindfulness
- Sleep mindfulness (this is done to prepare the body for sleep)

CHAPTER 11

Hope

"Let your hopes, not your hurts, shape your future."

—Robert H. Schuller

I HAVE SAID BEFORE THAT MY FAVORITE PART OF MY JOB IS THAT I GET to love everyone I work with. I get to sit with them and understand and love. I am not perfect at this, but for the most part, it happens naturally. This, along with being a parent, gives me a small but powerful understanding of how God sees us. We often hear that he understands, but I don't think we really know what that means.

It means he knows what it's like to be a pregnant teen who hasn't told her parents and is thinking of abortion because she is so scared.

It means he knows what it is like to have so much depression that getting out of bed is too hard most days. And how the shame doubles down because of that.

It means he knows what it is like to be overwhelmed as a mother—to love your kids so much and not know how to help them make all the right choices. He also knows how much shame we feel when we express more anger at our children than anyone else.

It means He knows what it is like being raised in a conservative community or religion and being gay. He understands the inner conflict that brings while experiencing mixed messages about how to live or love.

It means He knows what it is like to hate your body to wake up every day feeling like you are trapped in a shell that you hate and refuse to look at in the mirror. He knows how it feels to obsess over other people's bodies so much, because you feel like if you looked like them, then you could finally be happy.

It means He knows what it feels like to feel shame. To feel worthless. To feel not good enough.

For some, the idea of God's love is very literal, as it is given directly from a deity or heavenly being. For others, God's love might be experienced as shared energy that is divine. Either belief carries great meaning and depth. I feel something in between the two. Connecting with greater love can be so powerful. Love can take us to a place of empathy, to heal those holes in our hearts. Love can give us the courage to be open and honest about those things we need to do differently or what we need to do next in order to progress into a life with more hope and joy.

Honesty and Humility

There is a common misconception when it comes to humility. Some people take it to mean that they cannot think anything positive about themselves. That they are the "dust of the earth" and shall remain lowly. Thinking anything positive about the self is sometimes assumed to be boastful and prideful. I discuss this often when talking about self-love. People do not feel comfortable fostering self-love because it seems to be a form of pride. With these individuals, it is too much to ask them to tell me what they are good at or what their strengths are. There is nothing wrong with saying positive things about yourself that are true facts. Pride and conceit come in when we place ourselves higher than other people. I believe Christ would comfortably say positive facts about himself while maintaining complete humility. He could say, "I am a people person. I am great with kids. I am a good listener and I am kind. Also, I do well with public speaking." We can foster both self-love and humility.

However, there also needs to be an honest evaluation of self in order to really experience guilt. This may lead to the need for more humility. Relationships are a good place to find this need. Years ago, when my husband and I had been married just a couple months, we were settling into living with each other. Up to this point, I had only lived with women. I grew up with my four sisters and later had many female roommates. Other than my Dad, I had never lived with a man.

I thought I was pretty easygoing and that we were well-matched. That was true, but I still had very different expectations for how things should be done around the house. I found myself fixating on things Brady would leave out or not do according to my expectations. These would be simple things, like not putting away the cereal box, leaving a light on, or leaving his socks in the living room. Very simple things. But these simple things were adding up to become big things. I found myself cleaning up after him, more than I thought I should. I tried to talk to him about it. He was sweet and understanding and said he would try better. As time went on, I didn't see much change. Again, I was fixating and feeling frustrated.

One morning, I decided that I was not going to clean up after him. I was going to leave things as he left them and point them out at the end of the day. So I said, "Ok Babe, there are five things you didn't do this morning. I counted. You need to find what they are and fix them." I figured this was a good way to get my point across. It was a problem that needed to stop and I just had to practice a little "tough love." Well, it didn't go well. My poor husband felt attacked and hurt. My approach was not kind. I thought I was going to change his innocent, but naive, perspective of how things were supposed to be, and he would immediately be converted to my way of thinking—because it was obviously the right way. Then the rest of our marriage would include smooth, blissful cooperation for all the years to come. (Oh, the sweet naivety of a new bride.)

As a couple, we didn't argue much at all. Over the years, I have realized that is attributed to Brady and his non-confrontational approach. He is, and always will be, a peacemaker. So there we were, me being harsh and direct, the "You are doing it wrong, so change" dictator. He was blindsided by me shaming him. The things he was doing or not doing were not intentional. He had no idea there was anything wrong. Looking back, I have to laugh at how confused he must have felt. Luckily, I learned quickly that I needed to think and act differently.

I had to humble myself and understand how my behavior and way of thinking were not okay. If I was being honest, I would admit that I was more concerned with how I was feeling than how Brady was feeling. I could talk to him about my concerns and we could have open conversations, but he was certainly not the only one who needed to change.

The emotions attached to humility and honesty expose vulnerability; hence, the natural aversion to them. However, the entire experience of seeing ourselves fully is part of growth. One of the best ways we facilitate that is by confession. The idea of confession is common in many religious and therapeutic practices. Not that I agree confession is needed to the extent that it is often practiced. The general function of confession is interesting. In therapy, people are often at an emotional low point and part of feeling better includes telling someone about those emotions. Talking about things they have never talked about before. Two phrases show up in therapy on a regular basis: "I have never told anyone this before," and "I feel like a burden/weight has been lifted." It takes a certain level of humility to talk when shame is involved. It also takes courage to use that humility in order to understand the self better. There is a therapeutic quality to the act of putting everything out there. It is the combination of humility and courage that embodies truth.

These principles of guilt, honesty, confession, and humility are essential for anyone recovering from addiction. In order to truly heal from addiction and maintain stable sobriety, people must go through a long process of a complete, honest evaluation of themselves and how the addiction hurts them and those around them. Alcoholics Anonymous (AA) was the beginning of all 12-step programs. Because of their own experiences with alcoholism, Bill Wilson and Dr. Bob Smith started AA back in 1935. They joined together and dedicated themselves to serving other alcoholics as a way of maintaining their own sobriety. Up to that point, Bill Wilson had dealt with years and years of alcoholism, which damaged his career and family. He, being a very intellectual and motivated person, would try over and over again to quit and think he was done for good. Yet, he always found himself drinking again.

It wasn't until his second hospitalization and a life-changing reconnection with an old friend that he turned to God. He was able to give up his own plans to control his addiction and turn himself over to God and his will. Part of his change required him to make a list of all the people he had harmed and make direct restitution to them. He also committed to serving other addicts. Those ideas turned into the 12 steps that have guided over a hundred thousand groups all over the world and have been replicated for many other addiction disorders like narcotics, sex, overeating, gambling, and more. Some churches develop similar 12-step programs.

Step one is an honest acceptance that the person is powerless to overcome addiction alone. Step four requires the individual to take a personal moral inventory. AA literature explains step four as, "our vigorous and painstaking effort to discover what these liabilities in each of us have been, and are. We want to find exactly how, when, and where our natural desires have warped us. We wish to look squarely at the unhappiness this has caused others and ourselves. By discovering what our emotional deformities are, we can move toward their correction" (Smith and Bill W., *The Big Book Alcoholics Anonymous*).

Later, step five is, "admitting to God, to ourselves, and to another human being the exact nature of our wrongs" (Smith and Bill W., *The Big Book Alcoholics Anonymous*). This requires the individual to take the "moral inventory" created in step four and read and discuss it with a trusted friend. In later steps, the individual will make a list of people who have been harmed and will then make direct amends with those people. I love this idea of confession and making restitution. If you want to "work the steps," as they say, you must connect with people. You must connect and express your regret or guilt. That's exactly what I mean by shame resilience. Here is a set of people who are easily riddled with shame and as part of their treatment, they are supposed to connect with people, people who can truly empathize with them. It helps decrease the shame.

I have gone to several 12-step meetings before. My first was on an assignment for my addictions class in grad school. The groups are open to anyone who wants to come. Each group starts out with a welcome and then people take turns reading from the 12-step material, usually focusing on one step each week. After the reading, people can take turns sharing, if they want to. As I participated and listened, I was amazed at how refreshingly honest and authentic everyone was. The nature of the group strips people down to their raw selves as their defensive walls come down. For many, that may seem terrifying. The actual result is extreme love and connection. People usually have a home group they return to with the same people every week, because the bonds made through those vulnerable moments are valuable.

Another part of every AA meeting is the reciting of the Serenity Prayer. The full version of the prayer is given below. Often, the first four lines are repeated in an abbreviated form in each meeting:

> God, grant me the serenity
> To accept the things I cannot change,
> The courage to change the things I can.
> And the wisdom to know the difference.
> Living one day at a time,
> Enjoying one moment at a time;
> Accepting hardship as a pathway to peace;
> Taking, as He did, this sinful world as it is,
> Not as I would like it;
> Trusting that He will make things right
> If I surrender to His will;
> So that I may be reasonably happy in this world
> And supremely happy in the next.
> Amen. (Smith and Bill W., *The Big Book Alcoholics Anonymous*)

I keep a copy of this prayer in my office. I refer to it often with clients and with myself. I do not believe that God's work happens in only one place or with one group of people. The AA program was divinely inspired and has been bringing people to God for decades and helping them get sober. Interestingly, I've seen those who get the most out of their recovery with this program live it religiously. They attend meetings faithfully. They read the material as often as possible. They pray every day. They serve each other and try not to judge. They are assigned to sponsor or be sponsored by another group member. Most importantly, they put their faith in God as the one in charge of their lives.

CHAPTER 11: HOPE

My sister struggled with alcoholism for a long time. She found God at AA. Now, AA is her church. It has saved her in ways she could not find in any other religious setting. Yet, it was where God was waiting for her.

It's kind of funny that when I was in that first meeting (which met at a church), I noticed that everyone was holding these small, dark blue books. I could tell the books were well-read and used a lot because some were worn at the edges and the pages were highlighted all over. Some people even quoted the book during their turn. I had to do a double-take because I quickly thought, "Hey, do they have scriptures here? Those books look like scriptures!" In reality, I wasn't far off. The book is called The Big Book, and it's full of incredible material designed to give hope and support as addicts work their recovery.

This is a beautiful example of utilizing guilt to connect with God and heal from pain. People who struggle with addiction are flooded with shame, almost more than anyone else. There is no way they can even begin to recover if that shame remains unchanged. There is a vicious shame cycle that happens with addiction:

1. First, the person engages with the addiction (drinks, looks at porn, shops, gambles, and so on).

2. Next comes the shame. It can be so overwhelming that the person becomes extremely depressed and even suicidal.

3. Third, as a way to escape the shame, pain, and depression, the person turns back to the addiction for help coping.

It is often said in psychology that "all things are purposeful." Addiction serves a purpose. In most cases, addictions are a way of coping with other emotional struggles. The addiction usually provides a temporary numbing experience from the emotion (stress, depression, anxiety, sorrow, and/or shame). Again, this is where the power of guilt can break the cycle:

1. The person engages with the addiction.

2. They feel true guilt for their actions but feel motivated toward positive change.

3. They reach out for help, develop a new prevention plan and ask for forgiveness, repenting if necessary. They pray, connect with loved ones, address the depression in a better way, try to love more intensely, and encourage themselves. Essentially, they cope in a healthier way.

Addiction provides a great model to observe the influence guilt can have on change. With addiction, the source of guilt or shame is obvious. Other times, it may not be so clear. Guilt is important and acts as a signal to help us improve. I had a family member talk to me about some distress he was feeling about work. He writes:

> After almost every single interaction with a certain coworker of mine, I recognized the need to be kinder to this person. He had a very different way of going about things, so I treated him with impatience. It was these feelings that left me with a tangible weight upon my shoulders after I learned he died by suicide. I carried this weight with me for about a month before calling a family member who I have great trust in. She told me that rather than feeling full of shame, I should shift my mindset. The shift in mindset that she prompted helped me to see the guilt as motivation to treat everyone with the same patience and kindness that I was unable to give to this late coworker of mine. It was this mindset of viewing guilt as a motivational tool that helped me alleviate the tangible weight of shame.

Accountability and Motivation

What helps with motivation to do things differently? In tenth grade, I had an amazing math teacher that I loved dearly. She was a very "open book" and would talk to us about all sorts of things most teachers would not. Once she was talking to us about her recent colonoscopy and said that she needed to go on a diet. The best way for

CHAPTER 11: HOPE

her to stay motivated when she started something new, like a diet, was to tell everyone she knew about it. That way, she felt accountable to them. Even if they never asked about it, she knew they knew and that gave her the extra oomph to keep going. I will never forget that (especially because it was my first full briefing on what a colonoscopy was). I thought it was weird but also kind of genius.

For years, I was never really good at exercising. When I signed up for a race with friends or went to the gym with them, I maintained my motivation. There were people around me to keep me accountable. Similar to confession, accountability is another important principle of different religious and therapeutic systems. AA and many other 12-step programs have this "support role" built into their system. They call it a sponsorship. The process of becoming a sponsor and choosing a sponsor is kind of a big deal. There is actually a 20+ page pamphlet available to help this process go smoothly.

In therapy, a counselor can be somewhat of a coach who helps motivate, direct, and encourage people. I give "homework" assignments to my clients all the time. The intention is to help them integrate new ideas and behaviors into their everyday life and then, because they are accountable to me, they can return the following week and discuss how it went. Showing up every week, regardless of any change or progress, makes each week go better because they are connected and accountable to me. That can be a very powerful and motivating relationship.

Motivation is fascinating. There are those people who hit the ground running every day. They don't stop until the sun is down and the list is complete, and sometimes not even then. There are those who are lucky to get out of bed at all. This is usually the depressed population. There are people like me who ebb and flow from one to the other. There are days where, for whatever reason, I am in high gear the whole day and I plow through task after task. The feeling grows and multiplies as I work. It feels great. However, I have other days that feel like I'm moving through sludge all day long. I am still slowly working or doing things that need to be done, but it takes so much effort. At times I just sit, eyes staring off into nothing, wishing I could go back to bed or watch movies the rest of the day, or both. The allure of doing nothing is so tempting. I imagine most of us are like me. We have good days and bad days.

So what influences motivation? When it comes to guilt and growth, motivation is integral. Repentance is a process that requires action. We cannot repent, improve, or grow while "sitting down." Brendan Burchard is a high-performance coach and an expert in the field of motivation. His motto is "Live. Love. Matter." Beautiful ideas, right? He has found that the two important elements of motivation are:

1 Ambition—the desire to chase after something more.

2. Expectancy—the belief that you are capable of your ambition. (Buchard, *Motivation Manifesto*)

In my experience, ambition is not the problem. It's the expectancy. We often feel the ambition to improve. What we lack is the true belief that we can actually succeed. This is where shame hijacks the process. When I am assigning homework for therapy, the people who do not usually follow through lack the expectancy that they can really change and feel better. If I could give them a sure knowledge that if they did A, B, and C, they would feel less depressed and anxious. No one likes those feelings. They would be highly likely to follow through. At times, I do make those promises to people. I believe in the work and the therapy that helps change happen. My clients believe me, but they do not believe in themselves. If we feel guilt without shame, we need to believe that we can do hard things.

There is evidence that shows motivation is not innate. It is something we create. When we start moving and doing, we create momentum, which creates more energy to keep moving and doing. I experience this when I am doing housework or yard work. I start in one place and while I'm working, I find more things that need to get done. I think, "Why not? I'm already working, might as well get that done, too." There is less resistance to keep going because my momentum is high. I am the same way with my writing. Sometimes it takes time to get the "cogs" moving. Once I start writing and push through the initial beginning, my thoughts and ideas start flowing faster and better.

Since I worked with college students for the first seven years of my career, motivation was discussed a lot. There was one man I was working with who struggled with simply getting started. He was a good student and got good grades when he actually completed his assignments. He was a perfectionist, so the pressure to do it perfectly often kept him from even starting. One day I told him to just sit at his computer and start randomly typing. I said, "You don't even have to type actual words. Just get your fingers moving on the keyboard." In that way, I figured the initial movement would help the motivation kick in.

Hope and Fear

"Hope is the only thing stronger than fear." —Robert Ludlum

Amidst all the fear that shame incites, hope is a way through. Hope is the belief that shame is a lie. Even when we feel shame so strongly and feel overwhelmed with despair, hope is believing that what we feel is not truth. At some point, our body and mind will feel differently.

This links back to the physical reaction of the stress response. Maintaining a sense of hope can help regulate our limbic system and help our brains "turn back on." This is something I teach my kids. My son is a classic example of what happens. He often gets really worked up about things, whether it is a punishment or an argument with a sibling. He is very argumentative and nothing we say helps his understanding. Eventually, it gets so bad that he is either sent to his room or he chooses to go there on his own, fuming all the way down the hall. Then, and this happens almost every time, about ten or fifteen minutes later, he comes out more calm and says, "I'm sorry. I shouldn't have acted that way." For my son, when he is worked up, his brain is turned off and no information penetrates. He is a smart, kind kid, so when he calms down and his stress response dissipates, he can understand the whole situation better.

That is another reason why breathing is an important part of de-stressing. Breathing is the only regulatory system we can control. It helps balance the body and reignite the prefrontal cortex. Breathing turns the brain back on. Fear creates confusion in the body. Hope gets us through that confusion.

When we understand these concepts and can recognize when our body and mind are stuck in intense emotions, we can trust that what we are feeling is not true. Once we calm down or de-stress, we can see things more clearly. That's where hope comes back in. The New York Times published an interview with Desmond Tutu. In the interview, he said, "Hope is being able to see that there is light despite all of the darkness" (Solomon, "The Priest").

Faith

"Hope is faith holding out its hand in the dark." —George Iles

Spiritual support to keep going and not give up is a beautiful element of our progress in life. When we feel like it is too hard to keep trying, the momentum has stopped, the emotions and possibly the shame have become too much, and we just want to throw in the towel, Christ can give us hope that we can keep going and keep trying.

Back in Chapter Two, I talked about my burn. Because I was so young, this experience was not very traumatic for me. All the trauma that it caused belonged to my mother. She was a loving mother of her small child and was there, with full memory, for every moment of my pain. Toward the end of my physical therapy, she was at the point of losing all hope. Between my treatments and while still caring for my three older siblings, she was completely overwhelmed and emotionally empty. She wrote:

> It was all I could do to continue this terrible ordeal every day, and after an unbearable treatment on the tenth day, I drove home from the hospital in a pool of tears, feeling helpless and alone. As I drove, I became irrational. In my frantic state of mind, I decided to run away and hide my baby. I decided to take Erika away from any doctors, nurses and hospitals. I simply could not go back to the physical therapy another day.

CHAPTER 11: HOPE

In the midst of my tears, I suddenly began to feel the love of the Lord surround me and a spirit of hope began to fill the car. I knew a heavenly presence had come to me and I heard the Spirit of the Lord say to my heart, "Now you know how I feel when you are hurting and I can't explain that your suffering is for your good."
As I pondered what I had just experienced, I began to cry even harder. This time with a feeling of strength and assurance that I was not alone. A feeling of understanding poured over me and I realized that the Lord completely understood the pain we were enduring. He had endured it many times himself. In that moment, it was as if he had reached down from heaven and hugged me with his deepest compassion. I knew he wanted me to know that he was with us. His message to me came through loud and clear and brought me indescribable peace. I knew I would be able to endure the following days of treatment with Erika. I felt confident that she would have understanding and that someday I could explain to her that this was for her good. After that day, I returned to the hospital with Erika and completed the treatment with a clear understanding that all would be well. I knew this experience would be for our good.

For my mother, faith and hope made all the difference. They carried her through one of the most difficult times of her life.

Practice

- What experiences have you had that evoked more guilt than shame? Why was that different from your shame experiences?

- Fill out the motivation chart on the following page.

Areas where you are motivated	What helps that motivation?	What hinders that motivation?

Areas where you aren't motivated	What helps that motivation?	What hinders that motivation?

- When it comes to accountability, it is important to choose people you feel safe with emotionally. They need to be willing to encourage you to seek out change and help keep you on the path to wellness. Be aware of people who make you feel shame (even unintentionally). When experiencing accountability, it's important to feel comfortable being yourself. Who can you rely on for accountability when needed?

- Out of all the content covered in this book, what spoke most to you? Why do you feel like that was so important for you to learn/read?

- Who do you feel strongly connected to and why?

- Who do you want to connect more with and why?

- Is there anything about the connection you see differently after reading this book? What and why?

- How do you feel about yourself? Do you want that to be different?

- How is your understanding/experience of your shame different?

- Do you feel connected to yourself? Why or why not?

- What are your feelings about connection with God or a higher power after reading this book?

Final Practice

Here is a final mindfulness exercise you can do to fully assess your connection with others, God, and self:

Ideally, mindfulness is done while closing your eyes or resting them in one place. That makes it hard to read the directions and focus on your experience. Many mindfulness practices are guided, meaning someone is speaking the directions to you while you breathe and focus. By nature of this being a book, reading is essential. There are some ways to get around it. Someone could slowly ready the directions to you, pausing occasionally and allowing ample time to think and experience. You could record yourself reading the directions out loud. Or, you could simply read the directions first, then try to remember the ideas and do mindfulness afterward, relying on your memory to take you through the exercise.

Take a moment to settle into a comfortable spot. Let your eyes slowly close as you start to become aware of your breath and your body. Take several deep breaths and notice the sensation of the breath as it comes in and out of your body. Slowly breathe as deeply as you can, all the way to the bottom of your diaphragm. Slowly breathe out while allowing every spec of air to release from your lungs. Notice your chest rise and fall with every breath.

As you continue to breathe deeply, I want you to visualize yourself in a comfortable and safe place. This could be anyplace, real or imagined. A place you feel free to be yourself. A place that allows calm and presence. Allow yourself to notice what is around you. Are you outside or inside? What is your body position? How does it feel in your body to be there and observe this safe place? Are there sounds? Smells? Textures? Is it warm or cool?

Now, you see a person in your life with whom you feel very connected. He or she is a little way off and walking toward you. What do you feel as you see this person? You see a face that is warm and welcoming. What is it that makes you feel so close? How does this person feel about you? You start talking to each other. What do you talk about? Is there anything important you want to say? Is there anything important this person wants to say to you? How does it feel to talk and hear/say these things? You finish talking and bid farewell with a touch, either with a hug or grasping hands. What does it feel like to be touched in this warm way? What does it feel like as the person walks away?

After the first person leaves, someone new starts walking slowly toward you. This person is God, in whatever embodied character you envision. If, for whatever reason, that doesn't feel right, allow your mind to show you someone else who is uniquely close to your soul. Now, as the person walks toward you, notice what they look like. Short? Tall? How does it feel to be approached with such love and concern? What do you know about God or this special person? What feelings do you share? You are gently approached and engaged in conversation. Who speaks first? What is said? Is there anything you need or want to say? What does it feel like to be near? How does your body feel? You finish speaking and bid farewell with a touch. How does it feel to be touched in such a warm way? What does it feel like as you part company?

The second person walks out of view and another person slowly walks toward you. This is someone who knows you very well, more than any other person on earth. This person is you, many years older. What do you look like? How does it feel to look at your future self? How does that person feel while walking over? As the older you walks up to you, you talk. What do you talk about? Is there anything you need or want to say to say to your older, wiser self? Is there anything that would be said in return? What does it feel like to talk with and be

CHAPTER 11: HOPE

near the older you? How does your body feel? As you finish speaking, you say farewell with a touch. How does it feel to be touched in that warm way? What does it feel like as you part ways?

Before you leave this safe place, give yourself a moment to ponder these three conversations with these three important people. How do you feel now? What did you gain from those conversations? What does your body feel like? Breathe in this moment of awareness.

Now, allow your focus to come back to the breath in the present moment. Start to focus on your body in the space you are in now. Recognize the sensation of breath and the sensations in your body as you sit, stand, or lie down. How does your body feel now compared to before you did this exercise? Take several deep breaths and when you are ready, you can open your eyes.

Conclusion

WHETHER YOU ARE A BELIEVER IN GOD OR NOT, WHETHER YOU ARE a believer in any deity or not, to hope is to heal, move forward, and persevere. To hope for something good and better is an integral part of living. To recognize that we are not alone in our suffering, that suffering is a shared human experience. As we rely on ourselves, others, and God (or something greater than ourselves), it allows us to better access resilience and strength. We are powerful, valuable, worthy people. Our power connects us to each other and God. It's what gives us meaning.

Many people talk about finding the meaning of life. Maybe this is it.

Bibliography

Angelou, Maya, and Arthur Austen Douglas. *928 Maya Angelou Quotes.* CreateSpace Independent Publishing Platform, 2016.

Bianchini, Ana Paula, et al. "A Study on the Relationship between Mouth Breathing and Facial Morphological Pattern." *Brazilian Journal of Otorhinolaryngology*, vol. 73, no. 4, 2007, pp. 500–505., doi:10.1016/s1808-8694(15)30101-4.

Brasted, Chelsea, "Interview with Maya Angelou." Times-Picayune, 2013.

Brown, Brené. *Braving the Wilderness: the Quest for True Belonging and the Courage to Stand Alone.* Random House, 2019.

Brown, Brené. *Dare to lead list of values.* (2021, October 27). Retrieved July 3, 2022, from https://brenebrown.com/resources/dare-to-lead-list-of-values/.

Brown, Brené. *Daring Greatly: How the Courage to Be Vulnerable Transforms the Way We Live, Love, Parent, and Lead.* Penguin Books Ltd, 2015.

Brown, Brené. *The Gifts of Imperfection: Let Go of Who You Think You're Supposed to Be and Embrace Who You Are.* Hazelden, 2010.

Brown, Brené. "Listening to Shame." TED, www.ted.com/talks/brene_brown_listening_to_shame. Accessed 15 Jan. 2020.

Brown, Brené. "The Power of Vulnerability." TED, https://www.ted.com/talks/brene_brown_the_power_of_vulnerability?language=en.

BIBLIOGRAPHY

Burchard, B. (2014). *The Motivation Manifesto: 9 declarations to claim your personal power.* Hay House.

Call the Midwife. Season Holiday Special, PBS, 2017.

Chödrön, Pema. *The Places That Scare You: a Guide to Fearlessness in Difficult Times.* Shambhala, 2018.

Covey, Stephen R. *The 7 Habits of Highly Effective People.* FranklinCovey, 2016.

Dead Authors Society, 2016.

Dew, Sheri L. *No One Can Take Your Place.* Deseret Book, 2004.

Ermer, Chelsea. (n.d.). *Perspective.* Retrieved July 3, 2022, https://ermer.weebly.com/perspective.html.

Hurston, Zora N. *Their Eyes Were Watching God: A Novel.* London: Virago, 1986.

Kabat-Zinn, Jon, et al. "Jon Kabat-Zinn: Defining Mindfulness." *Mindful,* 11 Jan. 2019.

Lisitsa, E. (2022, June 16). "The Four horsemen: Criticism, contempt, defensiveness, & stonewalling." The Gottman Institute. Retrieved July 3, 2022, from https://www.gottman.com/blog/the-four-horsemen-recognizing-criticism-contempt- defensiveness-and-stonewalling/.

Lotz, Anne Graham. *The Magnificent Obsession: Embracing the God-Filled Life,* Participants Guide, 7 Sessions. Zondervan, 2010.

Lowell, Josh and Mortimer, Peter, directors. *The Dawn Wall.* Red Bull Films, Red Bull Media House, 2018.

Maltz, Maxwell, et al. *The New Psycho-Cybernetics: the Original Science of Self-Improvement and Success That Has Changed the Lives of 30 Million People.* Souvenir Press, 2012.

McKay, David O., and Woodger, Mary Jane. *The Teachings of David O. McKay.* Deseret Book, 2004.

Milton, John, 1608–1674. *Paradise Lost.* London and New York: Penguin Books, 2000.

BIBLIOGRAPHY

Monson, Thomas S. "We Never Walk Alone," *Ensign*, Oct. 2013.

Neff, Kristin. *Self-Compassion*. Hodder & Stoughton, 2013.

Nhãt Hạnh, Pagels, E. H., & Steindl-rast, D. (1995). *Living Buddha, Living Christ*. New York, Riverhead Books, MLA (7th ed.).

Rowling, J. K. *Harry Potter and the Deathly Hallows*. New York, NY: Arthur A. Levine Books, 2007.

Siegel, Ronadl. "The Great Courses." *The Great Courses*, Audible, 2001.

Smiley, Janelle. "Jannelle.smiley Hotel Bella Vista" Instagram. April 1, 2018, https://www.instagram.com/janelle.smiley/.

Smith, Robert Holbrook, and Bill W. *The Big Book Alcoholics Anonymous: the Story of How Many Thousands of Men and Women Have Recovered from Alcoholism*.

Solomon, Deborah. "The Priest." *The New York Times*, 4 Mar. 2010.

Stevenson, John, director. *Kung Fu Panda*. Paramount Pictures, 2008.

Talmage, James E. *Jesus the Christ: a Study of the Messiah and His Mission According to Holy Scriptures Both Ancient and Modern*. Valde Press, 2009.

Uchtdorf, Dieter F. "You Can Do It Now!" *Ensign*, Nov. 2013.

Wallace, David Foster, and Tom Bissell. *Infinite Jest: a Novel*. Back Bay Books/Little, Brown and Company, 2016.

About the Author

A glimpse into Erika's path through this life has included a lot of mountains, learning, loved ones, listening, and baths. Becoming an author was an unexpected cross path that included a lot more learning and baths.

Erika graduated with her bachelor's degree in outdoor recreation leadership and got her master's in counseling. After seven years of working for a university counseling center, she decided to start her own private practice. She is now in her tenth year as a clinical therapist and the good times keep rolling.

She has been married to her husband for nineteen years and together they have four rock star kids. In her free time she tries to fit in as much outside time with her family as she can. Someday she hopes to have enough time to binge more Netflix and true crime podcasts.

Notes